THE INDY AUTHOR'S GUIDE TO PODCASTING FOR AUTHORS

CREATING CONNECTIONS, COMMUNITY, AND INCOME

MATTY DALRYMPLE

WILLIAM KINGSFIELD PUBLISHERS

CONTENTS

"Set your course by the stars, not by the lights of every passing ship."
Omar Bradley

To the podcasters whose work has provided models of skillful sailing ...
Mark Leslie Lefebvre, Stark Reflections on Writing and Publishing
Joanna Penn, The Creative Penn Podcast
J. Thorn and Zach Bohannon, The Career Author and Writers, Ink
Dale L. Roberts, Self-Publishing with Dale
Jerri Williams, FBI Retired Case File Review

To the guests of The Indy Author Podcast, who have been kind enough to join me for a leg of my voyage.

And to my stalwart crew, Wade Walton and Mary Dalrymple, for their advice and support.

PART 1
THE PODCASTING VOYAGE

"Twenty years from now, you will be more disappointed by the things you didn't do than those you did. So throw off the bowlines. Sail away from safe harbor. Catch the wind in your sails. Explore. Dream. Discover."

SARAH FRANCES BROWN (NOT MARK TWAIN)

WHY PODCASTING ... AND WHY FOR AUTHORS?

"To anyone contemplating a voyage I would say go."

JOSHUA SLOCUM

My name is Matty Dalrymple, and I have hosted *The Indy Author Podcast* since 2016. I launched the podcast because I wanted an opportunity to talk with people in the writing and publishing communities about their areas of expertise, and to share that knowledge with my fellow independent authors.

When I left my corporate job in 2019 to pursue my writing and publishing work as a full-time career, podcasting expanded from a hobby to a key part of my non-fiction platform business strategy.

In the years since I launched my first episode, I have evolved not only my goals but also the approaches I take to achieve them. I have made and recovered from wrong turns. I have refined my processes and improved my results. In this book, I'll share the lessons I've learned along the way.

As those of you who listen to *The Indy Author Podcast* or have read my non-fiction work will know, I love using the nautical metaphor to explore the writing *craft* and the publishing *voyage*, so the Joshua Slocum quote with which I began this chapter is perfect for this book. If you are contemplating embarking on the podcasting voyage, I would say go—and in this chapter we'll explore the reasons why.

Why Podcasting?

Why is podcasting a platform that authors should consider?

Audio content is portable in a way that visual content is not. It caters to our crazily busy lives by enabling people to enjoy content while commuting to work, walking the dog, or folding the laundry. The technology to enable this access is expanding and improving every year—consider the ease with which you can sync your phone to your car's audio system and the explosion of the use of home audio technology such as smart speakers. Podcasting is a key facet of this audio-centric evolution.

Some statistics from Convince and Convert, which summarized the results of a 2020 Edison Research study of podcasting and other digital media, bear this out:

- 75% of Americans are now familiar with podcasting and 55% have listened to a podcast
- The number of podcast listeners has grown 37.5% in three years
- 37% of Americans listen to podcasts monthly, a number which has grown 54% in 3 years
- Weekly podcast listeners tune in to an average of six podcasts per week
- 76 million American homes are now equipped with smart speakers

As impressive as these statistics are, their focus on the US audience understates the potential global reach podcasts offer.

Of course, there have to be plenty of podcasts out there to meet such demand. According to Oberlo, quoting numbers from the Podcastinsights website, there are 850,000 active podcasts and over 30 million podcast episodes.

Your initial reaction might be, "With that many podcasts, what's the use of launching a new one?"

That's where our author mindset comes into play. As of mid-2020, there were over six million Kindle ebooks on Amazon, but we would never have become authors if our reaction to that statistic was to say, "If readers already have six million books to choose from, why should I add more to the pool?" We write our books and offer them to our readers because we're convinced that by honing our skills in our writing craft and by developing a professional approach to our publishing voyage, our efforts will enable our books to find an audience of enthusiastic readers.

As with books, so with podcasts. **By developing skills in the craft of podcasting, and by bringing a level of professionalism to the podcasting voyage, our efforts will enable us to find an audience of enthusiastic listeners.** In this book, I'll share my hard-won knowledge and experience in order to smooth your voyage into the waters of podcasting.

If you still need convincing about the value of podcasting, consider this quote from podcaster extraordinaire J. Thorn of The Career Author, host of Writers, Ink and The Author's Life Podcast (and past host of many more):

What moves the needle for me for everything, more than anything else, is podcasting. I know video is huge. I know YouTube is huge. I know there are people who are making fortunes on that and reaching massive audiences. But I still believe there's an intimacy to podcasting that doesn't exist in any other medium, including the written word. You are literally inside of someone's head. You can watch a video and be distracted and looking somewhere else, but with audio you're listening.

And if you think about it, it's so primal. It's what we did around campfires. We've only been writing for a little bit. We forget that writing is a very small part of our evolutionary process. It's relatively new and it takes a lot of cognitive energy to read something. But listening is what we've been doing for tens of thousands of years.

J. THORN, *THE INDY AUTHOR PODCAST*
EPISODE 45

The combination of rapidly evolving audio technology and the primal connection audio enables makes podcasting a powerful tool. But before we cast off and embark on our podcasting journey, let's examine what podcasting has to offer specifically for authors.

Why "for Authors"?

As the host of *The Indy Author Podcast*, podcasting for authors is a topic I can speak to from first-hand experience, and I'll offer several perspectives that I believe will resonate with my fellow authors.

First, I believe that for many of us, **a podcast is not an end in itself, but a route to a larger goal**—specifically, establishing connections within the writing and publishing worlds and building a community with listeners. These connections and communities are often a path to a further goal: income creation, either directly from the podcast or indirectly through other offerings, such as books or courses. These are the goals I have for my podcast, and I'll offer guidance to those with similar goals.

Second, for many authors, **the idea of putting ourselves out to an audience "over the air" might not be our natural tendency**. I don't want to lean too heavily on the creator-as-introvert stereotype. I'm not traumatized by crowds, and I've done plenty of talks in front of large audiences in my career (pre- and post-Indy Author). However, my natural tendency is always toward more solitary pursuits— for example, working on a book or a short story—and I believe that many authors share that tendency. Therefore, the tactics I've used to make the podcasting process positive and productive—despite my automatic preference for solitary work—are tactics I believe will resonate with other authors.

Third, podcasting requires **an intrinsically different relationship to your creative output and your audience than writing does**—a difference that may require authors to arm themselves with a different mindset.

- With writing, you can practice your craft with the comforting knowledge that, if the product isn't up to your standards, no one else need ever read it. With podcasting, you normally don't have the luxury of producing the equivalent of a rough draft.

- With writing, your readers might be happy with a new book every year or two. With podcasting, you'll never develop an audience if you produce a new episode that infrequently.
- With writing, you might have a policy never to read your reviews, and you should certainly have a policy never to respond to them (publicly, at least). With podcasting, engaging directly with your audience is a necessity.
- I have navigated both the writing and podcasting worlds and have found ways to make both work.

Plotting Our Course

In *The Indy Author's Guide to Podcasting for Authors*, we'll walk through the podcasting journey from the high-level strategies to the detailed tactics you can use to make sure your podcast is shipshape and Bristol fashion (in other words, in good order).

In Part 1 - The Podcasting Voyage, we've addressed the question "why podcasting?" and mentioned some of the author-specific considerations related to podcasting.

In Part 2 - Determining Your Destination, we'll look at three primary goals that are common among authors considering launching a podcast.

In Part 3 - Preparing for Your Voyage, we'll consider the type of "vessel" you want to use to take you to your destination —or, in less nautical terms, the strategies you will use to navigate your way to those goals.

In "Part 4 - Setting Sail," we'll examine some specific tactics you can use to make your podcasting voyage a smooth one.

These are mainly decisions that are made behind the scenes, and you can tweak them over time to better support your goals, or to accommodate shifts in those goals.

If you're excited about what the podcasting voyage offers you as an author, let's get underway—your destination lies ahead.

Captain's Log

As we review the various strategies and tactics related to hosting a podcast, it will be helpful for you to note your learnings and insights. At the end of each chapter, I pose a few questions for you to consider. Your responses will form your "Captain's Log," enabling you to note progress, acknowledge mistakes, and celebrate successes. It will serve as a guide as you steer your podcast through its voyage. When a course correction is needed, it will provide information you can use to adjust your bearing. A downloadable "Captain's Log" worksheet is available at TheIndyAuthor.com Podcasting for Authors.

The question for you to consider in this chapter is ...

What about podcasting as an author appeals to you?

Looking for a Pilot for Your Podcasting Voyage?

I love helping fellow authors embark on and succeed in their podcasting voyage, and if you go to TheIndyAuthor.com Podcasting for Authors, you can find lots of information on this topic, including my book *The Indy Author's Guide to Podcasting for Authors* and some free, downloadable resources. You can also find out more about my consulting services.

Using your answers to the questions included in the downloadable "Captain's Log," I work with you to **determine your desired podcasting destination, prepare for**

your podcast launch, and navigate your podcasting voyage.

Client Dr. John Dentico says:

Matty helped me understand the ins and outs of starting and sustaining a straightforward quality podcast, even when my original ideas and format were not the right mix. Her advice was invaluable, helping me simplify my approach and enabling me to produce a quality podcast.

If podcasting is a creative dream you want to pursue, I hope you'll allow me to join you on that voyage!

Go to TheIndyAuthor.com Podcasting for Authors for more information, and for other resources that can support your podcasting voyage.

PART 2
DETERMINING YOUR DESTINATION

"If one does not know to which port one is sailing, no wind is favorable."

LUCIUS ANNAEUS SENECA

DETERMINING YOUR DESTINATION - INTRODUCTION

"Without goals, and plans to reach them, you are like a ship that has set sail with no destination."

Fitzhugh Dodson's quote is a perfect one with which to begin a discussion of your goals for your podcast. Your voyage will be rough and circuitous if you set out without a clear idea of your destination.

Let's start by **examining some of the goals that a podcast can help you attain** so you can think through what you hope to achieve with your own podcast.

I started *The Indy Author Podcast* in 2016, driven mainly by two considerations. One was to have an excuse to talk with people in my immediate circle—people I had met through local author events or at writers' group meetings—about their areas of expertise. The other was a desire to repay the support I had received on my own author journey by sharing this knowledge with others. I published podcast episodes sporadically through 2018. In 2019, after leaving my corporate job, I moved to a more frequent schedule. In 2020, I began publishing episodes weekly.

As my podcast became more established and my approach

more well-defined, so did my goals, and I believe these are goals that other authors will share:

- **Establishing connections** with guests (beyond your existing, local circle of contacts) who are subject matter experts in the larger writing and publishing communities—relationships that can smooth your creative and professional journeys.
- **Building a community** among your listeners—a community that can support the goal of paying it forward to your fellow writers as well as providing a way of communicating with an interested audience about other offerings you might have, such as books, webinars, and online courses.
- **Creating income** either directly from the podcast itself (for example, through sponsorships or patronage support) or indirectly by using the podcast to build credibility for and direct listeners to your other offerings—money that can feed into the multiple streams of income that an indy creator must cultivate.

Your set of goals will be your north star for navigating your way to a successful podcast, so you should consider them carefully before you set out. Changing from one tack to another will disorient and disappoint listeners, who may abandon your podcast to seek the information they want elsewhere, meaning that you will lose some of your hard-won audience. That said, your goals may shift over time, as mine did, or external forces may suggest a change in direction. It's wise to reassess your goals periodically to ensure that any adjustments are intentional and well planned.

Captain's Log

You can capture your answers to these questions in the downloadable worksheet available at TheIndyAuthor.com Podcasting for Authors.

What are your goals for your podcast?
How do you foresee those goals might change over time?

ESTABLISHING CONNECTIONS WITH GUESTS

"Thought is the wind, knowledge the sail ..."

AUGUSTUS HARE

My original goal for *The Indy Author Podcast* was to provide an opportunity for me to **establish connections** with guests who were subject matter experts in the writing and publishing communities, to tap into the knowledge they had to share, then to make that knowledge available to others on the author journey.

My early interviews were with fellow members of the Brandywine Valley Writers Group. I was interested in finding out how a small press publisher differed from an indy author-publisher, so I spoke with Scott Pruden in Episode 3. I was interested in what opportunities short fiction offered, so I spoke with Tony Conaway in Episode 9. I was definitely interested in all the considerations that went into deciding to make the move to being a full-time writer, so I spoke with Ken Lozito in

Episode 11. By capturing what Scott, Tony, and Ken shared with me about their various areas of expertise, I was able to pass on that knowledge to the other members of the Brandywine Valley Writers Group, and perhaps even beyond.

As the podcast continued, I cast my net beyond my Brandywine Valley compatriots—for example, to fellow writers and subject matter experts I met at conferences. I spoke with Robert Blake Whitehill in Episode 8 about screenwriting; with Chris Grall in Episode 12 about mistakes writers make about firearms and how to avoid them; and with Wendy Tyson in Episode 15 about the five things she wished she had known before her books were published. The pool from which I was drawing expert guests was expanding, and so was the audience who benefited from their expertise.

With each guest and each connection I made in the writing and publishing worlds, the pool of potential guests continued to expand. I joined the New England chapter of Sisters in Crime and met the chapter president, Connie Johnson Hambley, with whom I discussed building a writer community in Episode 39. The connection with Sisters in Crime New England and with Connie led to an online introduction to thriller novelist Hank Phillippi Ryan, who in Episode 40 discussed storytelling lessons from her award-winning investigative reporting career. Hank's appearance on the podcast paved the way for other well-known authors to accept invitations, including Steven James, who in Episode 43 discussed twelve sure-fire ways to kill suspense in your novel. A charming story Steven told about novelist Robert Dugoni's daughter led to an appearance by Robert in Episode 47 to discuss flashbacks and backstory.

This partial list of some of my early podcast guests illustrates that the opportunities for establishing connections through your podcast is a virtuous cycle, with each guest and each connection opening a network of new paths for you to pursue. Even better, these new paths will benefit your listeners as well as you.

You can encourage this virtuous cycle by asking each guest at the end of your interview if there are other topics or guests that they feel would be right for your podcast. Those who are established authorities in their field are likely to recommend others of a similar standing, so once you have reached the point of getting to speak with your most desired guests, you will more easily be able to find more of the same.

This turns your podcast into a valuable networking tool for yourself, your guests, and your audience. If you like and follow your guests on social media, they will often like and follow you back. If a guest makes a positive reference to another person in your industry, notify that person of the mention. If a particular episode has an especially large number of downloads, let the guest know that.

Look for opportunities to keep the connection alive—don't just sail on to your next episode or interview without a backward glance. (We'll discuss this in more detail in the chapter "Making the Most of Your Content.")

As you nurture your connections with your guests, you lay the foundation for a second goal: building community with your audience.

Captain's Log

You can capture your answers to these questions in the downloadable worksheet available at TheIndyAuthor.com Podcasting for Authors.

Who are your "most desired" guests for your podcast?

BUILDING COMMUNITY WITH LISTENERS

"The thing I realized this last few days is that the earth is a big place."

PAUL CAYARD

One of the most powerful aspects of podcasting is that the earth is your potential venue—most podcast platforms provide global reach—and it is indeed a big place. As enjoyable as chatting with your guests will be, it's an empty pursuit without an audience to benefit from it. A growing audience will be an attraction to encourage your most desired guests to accept your invitation, and once they do accept your invitation, you have the opportunity to expand your audience to their fans and followers.

The first step to building a listenership is to be a listener yourself. Just as being an enthusiastic reader is a prerequisite for being a successful writer, so is **being an enthusiastic podcast consumer a prerequisite for being a successful podcast creator**. You can learn valuable lessons about how to shape your own podcast by assessing those you enjoy ... and you can learn valuable lessons about how *not* to shape your podcast by assessing those you dislike. As a listener, you learn what the podcast conventions are, not necessarily so that you will follow them blindly, but so that you will understand when you are deviating from those conventions.

You will also gain personal experience with the type of connection that a successful podcast can create. I agree with J. Thorn's belief that "there's an intimacy to podcasting that doesn't exist in any other medium." I feel connected to the podcasters to whom I listen regularly in a way I would never feel if I read their blogs or followed them on social media.

The relationships you develop with your audience will be among the most valuable benefits you will gain as a podcaster. Your audience is a pool of similarly minded people to whom you can pay it forward with knowledge, insight, and community. The podcast platform means you can bring value to many more people than you could if you were to try to provide support to one person at a time. If your content is evergreen, you can use it over and over as the questions and issues it addresses arise among your audience.

If you provide your audience with quality content delivered in a professional manner, and if you demonstrate you are working not only to meet your own goals but to pay it forward to your community, you pave the way to achieving a third goal: creating income with your podcast.

Captain's Log

You can capture your answers to these questions in the downloadable worksheet available at TheIndyAuthor.com Podcasting for Authors.

What are your favorite podcasts, and what about them makes them so? How can you act on that knowledge for your own podcast?

What are podcasts you've tried and abandoned, and what prompted you to do so? How can you act on that knowledge for your own podcast?

More Resources

The Indy Author Podcast Episode 34 "Connecting through Video with Dale L. Roberts"

Links to the following resources are available at TheIndy-Author.com Podcasting for Authors:

9 Things Career Authors Don't Do: Podcasting by J. Thorn

CREATING DIRECT INCOME WITH YOUR PODCAST

"If your ship doesn't come in, swim out to it."

JONATHAN WINTERS

One of the many things I most appreciate about The Creative Penn Podcast is Joanna Penn's unabashed acknowledgment of the importance to a professional creative career of actually earning money—and not just enough to afford a cold garret, but enough to support the life you want to lead. I also appreciate Joanna's emphasis on the importance of multiple streams of income for the creative professional, and a podcast can be a valuable contributor to those streams.

One of the benefits of earning direct income from a podcast is that it's **scalable**. Unlike an editing service, for example, where your income potential is limited by how many editing jobs you can take on, you may need to do little more work for a podcast audience of a thousand than for an audience of ten, although your earning potential could well be a hundred times as much.

However, to set our expectations accordingly, I also want to acknowledge J. Thorn's caveat to his comment in Episode 45 of *The Indy Author Podcast* that "what moves the needle for me for everything, more than anything else, is podcasting":

The tricky part is that podcasting is a long tail game. Most people quit after seven episodes because no one's listening. And the reality is it takes months—more like years—to build an audience.

And, I would add, even longer to make your podcast a money-making venture.

However, if you're willing to put in the work and the time, podcasting can be an income generator.

Most podcasts are free to listen to, so you may be wondering how they can create income. There are two ways to monetize your podcast: directly (for example, through patronage, affiliate income, and sponsorships) and indirectly (by introducing your audience to other products or services you offer). We'll address direct income generation in this chapter and indirect income generation in the next chapter.

As of the writing of this book, most of the income created by *The Indy Author Podcast* is in the form of patronage—in my case, via Patreon and Buy Me a Coffee.

Patronage - Patreon

Patreon is a membership program that enables supporters to pledge a monthly contribution, usually small, to support creators. Those contributions are usually acknowledged by patrons-only offers such as merchandise, exclusive content, membership to private forums such as Facebook groups, or early access to material. Patreon is a great option for regular listeners of your podcast who want to support your efforts on an ongoing basis via automatic contributions.

If you pursue patronage as an income creation strategy, one decision you will need to make is what you'll offer patrons to thank them for their support. You will also need to decide if you'll have multiple membership tiers, each of which will require its own set of offerings. Be sure to weigh the costs—in time, money, and effort—of providing these.

- You can fairly easily assess the cost and benefit of **merchandise offers**: if a patron receives a branded T-shirt that costs you $20 to produce and ship only after they've been a patron long enough to have contributed more than $20, you are at least not losing money. However, you are significantly cutting into the income you're earning from that membership. I don't offer any merchandise to patrons of *The Indy Author Podcast*, not only because I don't think the cost-benefit is favorable, but also because I believe that in general people aren't interested in acquiring more stuff.
- **Patron-only podcast episodes or blogs** are popular offerings, but as with any of your work as an author, you have to factor in the cost in time and effort—and what else you might do with that time and mental energy. *The Indy Author Podcast* already takes more time from my fiction writing than I would like, so I've decided against patron-only episodes as an offering.

- Access to a **private social media group** can be a less time-consuming offer to maintain over time, especially if you offer access to a group you already manage. You can further control the time commitment needed from you to maintain this offering if you can create an environment in which members interact with, and provide value to, each other, rather than relying on you to provide all the interaction and value. Consider, though, that it will take some work on your part to establish that environment. (See the chapter "Making It Interactive" for more information.) I originally offered patrons of *The Indy Author Podcast* access to a private Facebook group, but I moved to Slack because I believe it provides a better environment for interactions among members that will make the group more self-sustaining.
- One offering that requires little additional effort is **early access to content** you will make public at a later date. For example, you could provide your patrons with access to your podcast episodes a few days before they go live on the podcast platforms (Patreon makes this easy to do). If your podcast has a video component, you could initially post the videos on a platform like YouTube as unlisted and provide patrons with links to enable them to access that content before it becomes public. You could offer Advance Reader Team access to your books through a platform like BookFunnel.
- The least costly offering, and the one that can be the most satisfying for both the podcaster and the patron, is a **public acknowledgement of the**

patron's support. I thank every new patron by name in the introduction of episodes of *The Indy Author Podcast*.

A final consideration for a patronage program is that offerings you extend to your patrons are by definition offerings that you are *not* extending to your non-patron audience. Weigh the potential income-creation benefits of exclusive membership against the benefits of inclusive listenership, as we will discuss further in the chapter on "Creating Indirect Income with Your Podcast."

I periodically tweak my patron offerings, but at the time of this writing, I offer three membership tiers for supporters of The Indy Author.

The entry-level tier ("The Indy Author Crew") provides:

- Inclusion in a patron list at TheIndyAuthor.com with a link to the patron's website
- On air thank you on The Indy Author Podcast
- Early access to the interviews on YouTube
- Access to a private Slack community

The mid-level tier ("The Indy Author Mate") adds periodic virtual meetings with other patrons and podcast guests on topics related to the writing craft and the publishing voyage.

The upper level tier ("The Captain's Club") adds ebook versions of *The Indy Author's Guide to Podcasting for Authors* and *Taking the Short Tack: Creating Income and Connecting with Readers Using Short Fiction*, plus early access to any future non-fiction books if the patron is active at the time of launch.

Patronage - Buy Me a Coffee

Another option for patron income is **Buy Me a Coffee**, which enables supporters to make contributions via PayPal or Stripe. Like Patreon, Buy Me a Coffee supports recurring donations, but for *The Indy Author Podcast*, I position it as a mechanism for occasional donations—for example, if a listener gets special value from a particular episode.

The only special offering I extend to Buy Me a Coffee patrons is to thank them by name in the podcast introduction. This is because the expectation is that they are using the contribution to acknowledge a benefit they have already received, such as information from a specific episode or even content on my website. I include the Buy Me a Coffee button in the footer of my website so that it's easy to direct listeners to "scroll to the bottom of any page at TheIndyAuthor.com" to buy me a virtual coffee.

Affiliate Income

There is a pool of author tools and resources that I couldn't do without—the Alliance of Independent Authors, Draft2Digital, Scrivener, Vellum—and I wholeheartedly recommend them to other authors. For these types of resources, when I have the opportunity, I become an affiliate of that company or product, and a podcast can be a way of boosting this affiliate income by introducing these products to a wider audience.

Part of each episode's pre-interview content is a "recommended resources," and these are often (but not always) affiliate products. In addition, if the guest or I mention one of those products during the episode, I'll post my affiliate link in the show notes, with the appropriate disclosure about my affiliate relationship—for example, "I love ALLi (or Draft2Digital or Vellum) so much, I'm an affiliate!"

Another affiliate opportunity is with Amazon, which enables you to earn affiliate income for any product that Amazon offers. As an added bonus, you earn commissions not just on the linked product, but on any other product that the shopper purchases at the same time as the linked product. As with any affiliate link, you must disclose your affiliate relationship with Amazon, and be aware that you may turn off some people by directing followers to that platform. You need to weigh the pros and cons for your own situation.

I strongly believe that you should present affiliate links only for products and services that you actively use, that you actually endorse, and that make sense for your audience—in my case, the tools I rely on as an indy author and publisher. Otherwise you risk, at best, confusing your followers about what your focus is or, at worst, causing them to view your podcast as a money-grab.

We'll discuss the importance of making sure that affiliates you promote are compatible with your topic and your branding in the chapter "Choosing Your Livery (a. k. a. Branding)."

Sponsorships

Unlike an affiliate recommendation, where you earn money when members of your audience purchase the recommended item, sponsors pay you to make the recommendation (and of course count on your audience members to purchase their product or service).

As with affiliates, when deciding what companies to approach about sponsorships, make sure that their products make sense based on your topic area, that their brand is compatible with yours, and that the sponsored products will provide value to your audience.

Companies assess sponsorships based on podcast reputation, number of downloads, and other factors that may not count in your favor when you're starting out. Therefore, you may want to pursue smaller, less well-known companies at the start of your podcasting voyage, then expand to larger, more well-known companies as your audience grows. However, don't discount the idea of probing for interest with your ideal sponsors, and if your first pitch doesn't pan out, follow up again as your metrics improve.

An alternative to asking for payments for sponsored recommendations is to barter services for mentions. Ask the company to provide you with the product free of charge in exchange for recommending it to your listeners. Keep in mind that if you find that you can't continue recommending the product—perhaps your needs change, or the product isn't one you feel comfortable promoting—you need to let the company know.

There are pros and cons to sponsorships. The pro is that for most podcasters, sponsorships provide a more anticipatable (although not necessarily larger) stream of income than affiliate income, at least for the duration of your contract. The con is that you are tied to the terms of your sponsorship for the duration. So, for example, if you fall out of love with the sponsored product, you're in a sticky situation. It's also more difficult to tailor a sponsor pitch to match the content of a particular episode.

For a more extensive discussion of sponsorship opportunities and how to pursue them, check out Episode 34 of *The Indy Author Podcast*, "Connecting through Video with Dale L. Roberts," starting at about 40:00.

Captain's Log

You can capture your answers to these questions in the downloadable worksheet available at TheIndyAuthor.com Podcasting for Authors.

Is direct income creation a goal for your podcast?

If yes, which of the direct income creation strategies we've discussed—patronage, affiliate income, and sponsorships—will you pursue?

If you're interested in affiliate income or sponsorships, what relationships will you pursue?

More Resources

The Creative Penn Podcast with Joanna Penn

The Indy Author Podcast Episode 34 "Connecting through Video with Dale L. Roberts" 40:00

The Indy Author Podcast Episode 45 "Nine Things Career Authors Don't Do: Exercise with J. Thorn"

Patreon patron membership platform

Buy Me a Coffee patron membership platform

CREATING INDIRECT INCOME WITH YOUR PODCAST

"The goal is not to sail the boat, but rather to help the boat sail herself."

JOHN ROUSMANIERE

Another income creation strategy, in addition to using podcast patronage, affiliates, and sponsorships for direct income (as discussed in the previous chapter), is to use the podcast to direct your audience to other income-generating offerings. The intimacy that is such a key factor in the draw of a podcast makes it a perfect vehicle for introducing listeners to your other products or services, assuming you have behaved in a way that has earned their trust. I can certainly attest to this through my behavior as a podcast listener. When a podcaster I follow has a new resource on offer—a book or an online course, for example—I'm willing to make the investment in those, having developed a trust in their expertise and their perspectives through their podcast.

A great example of this is J. Thorn's series *9 Things Career Authors Don't Do*, which J. and I discuss in Episode 45. The topics of that series, such as exercise and personal finance, are ones covered in many books, but J. has an enthusiastic audience who is interested not in learning generally about exercise or personal finance, but in hearing what J. and his collaborators have to say about those topics. In fact, J. is specifically targeting the audience that he and Zach Bohannon built up around The Career Author Podcast. They established credibility with the valuable information they provided to their listeners, and the trust they built gives them a ready-made audience for their other work.

Another great example of indirect income creation is Jerri Williams' use of her podcast *FBI Retired Case File Review* as content marketing for her books. Jerri served for 26 years as a special agent of the FBI, working major economic fraud investigations, and she focuses everything in her content universe—her podcast, her crime fiction, her non-fiction books, her email newsletter, and her listener offerings—on the theme of the FBI, its procedures, and its portrayal in books, TV, and movies. By keeping her podcast aligned on these topics, she naturally creates interest in the content that is her focus for income-generation: her books. She carefully planned this from the start:

"If you decide to do a podcast, the number one thing that you need to ask yourself is: *Are the people who will be listening to my podcast the same people who will be reading my books?* And if the answer is no, then your podcast is not going to be content marketing for your books."

Furthermore, Jerri makes her books available in a format that is sure to appeal to podcast listeners: audiobooks. Jerri hires an actress to perform her crime fiction, but she narrates her non-fiction work herself, capitalizing on that intimacy that audio provides.

In my own business, I earn more from consulting and speaking engagements and articles related to podcasting for authors than I do from podcast patronage or even from sales of this book! The podcast and book are more productive as business cards for those other offerings than money-makers themselves. I promote my consulting offering on the podcast and have also included a reference to it in this book as an additional resource.

If monetization through indirect income is a goal for your podcast, consider how this will play out for the podcast topic area you have in mind. If you offer products or services that are complementary to the topic of your podcast, you can cultivate an eager audience for those through your podcast. A promotion for this book is certainly appropriate for *The Indy Author Podcast* audience, with its interest in the publishing voyage.

In contrast, consider podcasts focused on fiction. This may seem like a natural topic for an author-hosted podcast, but there is little to offer listeners other than the book under discussion, or other books by the same author. Even J. Thorn's recommendation of podcasting as "what moves the needle" for him includes this caveat:

If you're interested in writing nonfiction or teaching or doing anything **that isn't fiction related**, I still think podcasting is the way to go.

J. THORN, *THE INDY AUTHOR PODCAST*
EPISODE 45

I believe the reason for this is that fiction-based podcasts create a connection between the audience and the guest, not between the audience and the host. I might listen to a fiction-focused podcast episode because an author I admire or know is the guest, but I rarely then subscribe to the podcast. Although I'll follow the author to other podcasts, I'm unlikely to follow the podcast host to other authors.

Your income creation goals—direct and indirect—will be tied to the strength of the relationship you build between yourself and your audience, not the relationship you build between your guests and your audience. Factor in this consideration when choosing your podcast topic area.

Captain's Log

You can capture your answers to these questions in the downloadable worksheet available at TheIndyAuthor.com Podcasting for Authors.

Is indirect income creation a goal for your podcast?

If you're interested in indirect income creation by using your podcast to introduce your audience to your other offerings, what are those offerings, and do they tie logically to the proposed topic of your podcast?

More Resources

The Indy Author Podcast Episode 45 "Nine Things Career Authors Don't Do: Exercise with J. Thorn"

The Indy Author Podcast Episode 51 "Podcasting as Content Marketing with Jerri Williams"

PART 3

PREPARING FOR YOUR VOYAGE

"You are the master of your own ship, pal."

EVEL KNIEVEL

PREPARING FOR THE VOYAGE - INTRODUCTION

"The planning stage of a cruise is often just as enjoyable as the voyage itself, letting one's imagination loose on all kinds of possibilities. Yet translating dreams into reality means a lot of practical questions have to be answered."

JIMMY CORNELL, *WORLD CRUISING HANDBOOK*

Before you embark on your voyage, it's best to step back and take an overarching view of your upcoming journey. If you're taking passengers across a lake in your bowrider, you'll want to know whether a straight route from point A to point B will be best, or if currents or wind suggest a more indirect route. You'll want to know if a slight detour might provide an especially beautiful vista or the chance to see some interesting wildlife. And you'll want to know from boaters who have crossed the lake before you what hazards lie under the surface, and how you might best avoid them. **You'll want to establish the**

strategy for your voyage to increase your chances of reaching your destination safely and of enabling you and your passengers to enjoy yourselves along the way.

In Part 3 - Preparing for the Voyage, we'll consider the experience you want to create for your audience: the topic of your podcast, the format and medium in which you'll provide it, on what schedule, and with what deliverables. We'll also look at how you can tie all these aspects together: through branding, or what I refer to in my nautical metaphor as your podcast's "livery." These are decisions that will be audience-facing, so you should hone them as much as possible before you embark on your podcasting voyage.

Captain's Log

You can capture your answers to these questions in the downloadable worksheet available at TheIndyAuthor.com Podcasting for Authors.

In addition to this book, what are some other podcasting resources you might tap into as you prepare for your voyage?

CHOOSING YOUR TOPIC

A decision you have no doubt already considered is the general topic of your podcast.

When I established *The Indy Author Podcast* in 2016, I defined the topic as *the writing craft and the publishing voyage*, and the name of the podcast suggested I was targeting independent author-publishers. However, the podcast did address topics more applicable to the traditional publishing world, such as how to write a query letter. My logic was that even authors pursuing a traditional publishing career should bring an indy mindset to their voyage to maximize their success.

I recognize that the podcast name might cause traditionally published authors to scroll past *The Indy Author Podcast* when searching for content related to the writing craft or the publishing voyage, so I'm finding ways to clarify an emphasis on *indy mindset* rather than *indy publication*. For example, when I have a traditionally published author, or other denizen of the trad world, as a guest on the podcast, I ask them to help spread the word about the podcast to their trad pub friends and colleagues.

A broad topic like *the writing craft and the publishing voyage* extending over both the indy and traditional worlds provides a lot of latitude in topic selection. It also means that I'm not likely to get bored with the topic. Consider, though, that **as podcasts continue to proliferate, there could be benefits to defining your topic more narrowly**. Niching down on a specific area—perhaps *the writing craft of short fiction*—theoretically narrows your pool of interested listeners, but it is still a huge pool, especially since podcasting enables you to reach a global audience.

A narrowly defined topic means that there are fewer other podcasts competing for your target listener pool, and the bond you can form with those listeners will be stronger based on the specificity of your shared interests. It also means that over time you could become *the* podcaster associated with your topic—for example, *the* go-to resource for *the writing craft of short fiction*—which could be a great brand booster. I wouldn't discount the possibility that, over time, I might migrate toward a more narrowly defined topic area if input from my listeners, or my own interest, suggests that.

Deciding to niche down on your podcast topic area still provides you with plenty of latitude regarding the topics you address. For example, targeting your podcast to *the writing craft of short fiction* doesn't mean that you can't address craft topics that would also apply to longer fiction or even to non-fiction, just that you need to keep the needs of your short fiction audience uppermost in your mind. Just make sure that a narrower topic is one that will hold your interest beyond a half dozen episodes, because if it will hold your interest, it will hold your audience's interest as well.

Your choice of topic will also influence to what

extent you will be able to repurpose the content, and over how long a time it will be useful to your audience. If you focus on an evergreen topic such as *the writing craft of short fiction*, you can still share that content, and your audience can still benefit from it, years later. If you choose a more time-bound topic, such as current events or rapidly changing technology, that information might be outdated in months or even weeks.

A way to test the longevity of your topic and of your interest in it is to hold the launch of your podcast until you have several episodes recorded. That will give you a good gauge of whether your chosen topic, and the podcast in general, is something you're enthusiastic about pursuing for the long haul.

You also want to consider all the different outlets, formats, and venues that your chosen topic area could play in. Jerri Williams provides a model of aligning all the content she produces around one topic area.

> "If you go to my website, you'll see my logo and then you'll see *true crime fiction*. My blog is about crime fiction. My podcast is about true crime and my books are crime novels that pull from true FBI cases. I really have thought a lot about this."
>
> JERRI WILLIAMS, *THE INDY AUTHOR PODCAST* EPISODE 51

The fact that Jerri aligns her work so clearly with her FBI expertise means that hers is the first name that springs to mind should anyone need expert information on FBI topics. In fact, several TV networks have engaged Jerri to act as a consultant for their FBI-focused shows.

Episode Topics

Although determining your episode topics will be a never-ending—and ideally enjoyable—task, it's helpful to think through in advance what these might be. In the Captain's Log for this chapter, I'll ask you to identify two dozen topics which might form the basis of individual episodes. The intent is not to tie you to these topics, but to ensure that even a niched-down podcast topic area will provide sufficient fodder for a half year's worth of weekly episodes, reducing the risk of a podcast that fades away—podfades—due to lack of material.

Your early episodes will be a "shakedown cruise" to test out the strategies and tactics you have planned for your podcast, and one of these will be appropriately matching the scope of a specific episode topic to your target episode duration. For example, for a podcast targeting *the writing craft of short fiction*, framing an episode topic as *advice on how to write effective short fiction* is too broad, and will result in a meandering and unfocused conversation. On the other hand, framing the episode topic as *best practices related to providing backstory in short fiction* might be too focused, and the guest might exhaust their thoughts on the topic in just a few minutes. Of course, if this topic is a specific area of study for the guest, they may be able to talk about it for hours, but you also need to consider if your audience will stay interested over that time.

Captain's Log

You can capture your answers to these questions in the downloadable worksheet available at TheIndyAuthor.com Podcasting for Authors.

What is the topic upon which you want to base your podcast?

What are two dozen topics which might form the basis of individual episodes?

CHOOSING YOUR FORMAT

Another key decision you will need to make is the format of your podcast—in other words, how many hosts and how many guests in what configuration.

It was easy for me to eliminate the formats that I knew weren't right for me personally or for my topic. Since I wanted to retain complete control over the process and product, co-hosting was unappealing, regardless of the opportunity it might provide to share the workload. Another disadvantage of co-hosting, from my perspective, was that all the participants would need to buy in to the destination and the course of the podcast voyage. Otherwise, I would risk having co-hosts working at cross purposes behind the scenes, and perhaps even on the episodes themselves. Furthermore, as a listener I find roundtable podcasts annoying, perhaps a matter of too many captains on the bridge. I rarely listen to a podcast hosted by more than two people without wishing that one or more of the ones I consider extraneous would drop out. However, for some prospective podcasters, having a co-host or two might be a method to avoid podfade because you would feel a responsibility to your podcasting partners to keep focused on and committed to your endeavor.)

A solo show also seemed like an awkward fit for me, not least because one of my goals in starting a podcast was the chance to **establish connections** with others in the writing and publishing worlds. Even if this hadn't been such a key goal, I had no interest in conducting an extended monologue with myself each week. Another mark against this format was that I didn't have an established persona that would draw listeners to a solo podcast.

There are other formats—panel, non-fiction storytelling, theater, or repurposed content—but none of these fit well with my goals for my podcast.

Formats that I rejected might seem exactly right for what you want to achieve. If one of these strikes your fancy, a quick internet search will identify popular examples of each format, and you can sample these to see if they seem like the right fit for you.

Since another driver of my podcast plans was the ability to interact one-on-one with subject matter experts so that my audience and I could benefit from their expertise, the **interview format** best fit my goals. Being a solo host meant all the work was on me, but I also got to be the captain of my vessel, which appealed to my indy spirit and my desire to exercise complete control over the material. An interview format also had the benefit not only of providing an opportunity to expand my connections with podcast guests but also of extending my potential reach into the listener community by attracting the attention of my guests' fans and followers as well.

If you are considering an interview format, think about whether you enjoy talking to other people about their area of expertise. This may seem obvious, but I've heard interview podcasts in which the host didn't sound particularly interested in what their guests had to say, and I didn't listen to them for long.

Occasionally an episode of *The Indy Author Podcast* will drift toward a **conversational** format. Unlike the interview format, where I am prompting guests to share their areas of expertise, in a conversational episode, the guest and I each participate more or less equally in a discussion about a topic of mutual interest. One example of an episode using the conversational format was Episode 19 "Judging a Book by Its Cover," in which my fellow crime fiction author Jane Gorman and I discussed our insights and lessons learned about book cover design. Neither of us is an expert in book cover design, but both of us had experiences we felt would be valuable to share with other authors, and the conversation was much more a two-way interaction than a question-and-answer.

Captain's Log

You can capture your answers to these questions in the downloadable worksheet available at TheIndyAuthor.com Podcasting for Authors.

Which podcast format most appeals to you, and why?

More Resources

Joshua Rivers' introductory *Podcasting for Authors Podcast* Episode 103 for another perspective on choosing your format—solo, interview, or roundtable—including the idea of morphing your format over time, or even mixing up the format from episode to episode

CHOOSING YOUR MODE, MEDIUM, AND VENUE

Three additional and somewhat related decisions you will need to make about your podcast are **mode** (live or recorded), **medium** (audio only or video), and **venue** (in person or virtual).

Mode - Live or Recorded?

I have never hosted a live podcast episode, but I have been a guest on several of them and I won't try to disguise my preference for a recorded podcast. What drives my preference?

- With a live broadcast, you can't easily recover from snafus, and these can encompass not only the minor inconveniences of life—a ringing doorbell, barking dogs, a sneezing fit—but the potentially more damaging issues of incorrect, misleading, or even unintentionally offensive statements you or your guest might accidentally make. **With a recorded interview, there is almost no problem**

that you can't address during the edit. If the interview is a total disaster, there's no need for the public ever to see it (although this situation should be rare, especially if you follow the advice in Part 4 - Setting Sail.

- With a live broadcast, guests must have as clear an idea of how the episode will play out logistically as you do. You don't want the guest to be unsure of when their mic is and isn't live, for example. That means the information you provide your guests will have to be extremely thorough and clear. **With a recorded interview, you just have to tell your guest to show up** on the video or audio conferencing and recording platform of your choice, and you can work out many of the logistical details with them before hitting *Record*.

- Because of the potential issues with live events, many people are uncomfortable with them and may not agree to do them, so you may limit your pool of potential guests if your podcast is live. **With a recorded interview, guests are more at ease**, knowing that if they really go off the rails, only you will ever know.

- One of the most significant downsides of a live broadcast is that it's difficult to focus your whole attention on your guest because, in the interest of avoiding dead air, you're inevitably thinking of the next question while the guest is responding to the previous one. **With a recorded interview, you can focus your full attention in the moment** because you know that you can always take a few extra seconds to regroup for the next phase of the discussion—seconds that you can edit out of the final product. Your guest will appreciate this attentive focus, and your audience will benefit from a better interview.

Medium - Audio-only or Video?

A somewhat similar consideration to the live or recorded question is whether to record in audio-only or in video as well. For *The Indy Author Podcast*, I like to interview my guests using video because **it's easier to build rapport over video**, and **easier to pick up body language** that will help you manage the conversation effectively. For example, you can tell if guests are silent because they're considering their answer to your question, because they're confused by the question, or because they've muted their mic while they get a drink of water. You get a better sense of when guests are wrapping up their answer, or if they are settling in for an extended discussion of the topic, and adjust accordingly. The availability of video also **expands your audience to video platforms like YouTube** and also **provides more fodder for promotional material**.

If you choose to provide video, consider if you're willing to make exceptions. There have been people I knew would be a great fit for *The Indy Author Podcast* and whose expertise I was eager to tap who didn't want to appear on video. In those rare cases, I agree to publish audio-only content. For social media promotion, I replace my usual video snippets with much shorter audiograms, which show the speaker's words displaying over an audio sound wave. Although these aren't as engaging as actual video of the guest, they do garner more attention on social media than still images do.

Even if a guest doesn't want video of the interview published, they are often willing to conduct the interview with video to gain the benefits of the smoother guest-and-interviewer interactions that video provides. Just be sure to confirm this with them in advance or be ready to turn off the camera if that will make them more comfortable.

A final component of the audio-video question, if you are recording both, is which you will optimize. Many more people listen to episodes of *The Indy Author Podcast* than view them, so I optimize for audio. That means that during the edit I might insert a pause to emphasize a transition from one speaker or topic to the next even though that means that the video momentarily goes black, or edit out pauses even if that makes the video look jumpy. Make your own decision based on the platform on which you want to optimize the experience.

Venue - In Person or Virtual?

For the early episodes of *The Indy Author Podcast*, when my guests were mainly members of the locally based Brandywine Valley Writers Group, I conducted the interviews in person. It may be easier to establish rapport with a guest in person, but in-person interviews have way too many downsides, the most significant of which is finding a location that works for you and your guest and that provides a reasonable recording environment (eliminating coffee shops and bars from consideration). You have the logistical complication of finding a time that accommodates not only the interview itself but also travel to and from that location by you and your guest, and of transporting your recording equipment.

A virtual interview via a tool like Skype or (my preference) Zoom is convenient for you and your guest and gives you the most control over the environment. But perhaps the strongest argument for a virtual venue is that you can draw guests from anywhere. If you're willing to conduct the interview in the middle of the night, you can as easily interview a guest on the other side of the world as in your own town.

Of course, you may be considering a podcast in which the location is intrinsic to its appeal—*Writers in Warehouses Talking Wordsmithing*—but factor in the logistical considerations about on-location recording before committing to that approach.

Captain's Log

You can capture your answers to these questions in the downloadable worksheet available at TheIndyAuthor.com Podcasting for Authors.

Will your episodes be live or recorded? What's the most important consideration for your choice?

Will your episodes be audio-only or video? What's the most important consideration for your choice?

Will your episodes be in-person or virtual? What's the most important consideration for your choice?

CHOOSING YOUR DELIVERABLES

A piece of advice that has stood me in good stead in my indy career was expressed by Voltaire as "the best is the enemy of the good" and by Confucius as "better a diamond with a flaw than a pebble without." Or, to tap into the nautical world, "better a simple dory on the water than a racing sloop on the drawing board." I like the nautical metaphor because it emphasizes that **you can adjust the effort you expend as long as you keep the quality of the product high**.

As you survey the podcast landscape, you might be tempted to do it all: to produce not only the podcast episodes themselves, but also transcripts complete with useful links and references, a presence on every audience-facing platform, snazzy promotional materials. However, by setting the bar so high in terms of the scale of your effort, you risk becoming overwhelmed and becoming one of those podcasters who never gets beyond the infamous seven-episode mark. A podcast with every possible auxiliary deliverable—the podcast equivalent of that racing sloop—might theoretically be "the best," but a no-frills audio-only podcast—that sturdily constructed dory—can be a resource that provides value to you and your potential audience ... and that actually takes you somewhere.

The Non-Negotiable Deliverable: High-Quality Audio

If you're launching your dory into potentially rough waters, you want to make sure it's watertight. If you're launching your podcast into the potentially rough waters of public opinion, you want to **make sure that your audio—the primary way people will consume your content—is similarly well-constructed**.

By well-constructed, I don't mean audio that would withstand the quality assurance assessment of an audiobook platform. I mean audio that is easy to listen to—free from distracting background noise, distortion, or volume variations. There are podcasts whose content I enjoy from which I have reluctantly unsubscribed because the audio quality was *not* easy to listen to. You don't want your podcast to be one of these. We'll be covering some tactics you can use to ensure that the listening experience is an enjoyable one for your audience in Part 4 - Setting Sail, and specifically in the chapter "Creating the Environment."

I also want to make a distinction between easy-to-listen-to audio and highly polished audio. Audio that is high quality from a technical perspective is a non-negotiable requirement of a good podcast, but you have some leeway in terms of how cleaned-up that audio is. I listen to podcasts where, as far as I can tell, almost no editing is done—all the inevitable pauses, repeats, and linguistic hiccups of conversational speech are left in. I also listen to podcasts (including my own) where most of the *um*'s and *you know*'s have been cleaned up. In general, I enjoy both, but once I develop an expectation about the approach a particular podcast has taken, a change to that approach can be jarring. Decide as early as possible how you will strike the balance between more natural-sounding content, which will require little or no editing, and more polished content, and the time involved in achieving that.

Everything Else

Beyond the core deliverable of high-quality audio, there is a seemingly endless list of other possible deliverables. Some might be part of the podcast itself, such as musical intros and outros or sound effects. Some might be supporting material, such as transcripts. Some might be promotional material, such as episode trailers or social media graphics.

My advice is to focus initially on the non-negotiable requirement of easy-to-listen-to audio and expand over time. If you start basic, listeners will be pleased when you add transcripts or more extensive show notes. If you start with all the bells and whistles, they will be disappointed if you end up having to scale back.

If you do want to offer some additional content, consider content that you are already creating as part of your podcast process. For example, listeners of Jerri Williams' *FBI Retired Case File Review* podcast can sign up for her newsletter in order to gain access to her "FBI Reading Resource"—a list of the books written by Jerri and her podcast guests. This is material Jerri would have available whether or not she shared it with her listeners. Just because content is easy to produce doesn't mean it won't be a valuable resource for your listeners. Consider what behind-the-scenes material might make sense for you to offer.

You don't need to pin down the exact deliverables you will provide before you launch your podcast, but you should consider the implications of what you're taking on. An example of a deliverable that I sometimes regret having introduced early in my podcast is the transcript. At TheIndyAuthor.com, I provide a full transcript of each episode, much of which I can produce using my audio and video editing software, Descript. Descript produces a fairly accurate transcript (and, best of all, editing the transcript creates the comparable edits in the audio and video as well).

However, the clean-up of the transcript can be time-consuming, especially when the guest or I reference obscure words, author names, book titles, or other material that Descript's transcription algorithms find hard to handle. I also have to make continuous decisions about whether to edit just the transcript or whether to have Descript make the comparable edits in the audio and video. For example, the guest or I might say "you know" as a filler phrase, and I don't want to include that phrase in the transcript, but in some cases it's better to leave the phrase in the audio and video because it sounds more natural and because editing it out will cause an awkward jump in the video.

Balancing the time required to create the transcript is the fact that some of my followers read the transcript rather than listen to the podcast, and it is a convenient reference for someone who wants to revisit a portion of the podcast they can identify by a specific word or phrase. It makes the content accessible to hearing-impaired followers. And over time, all that transcript content will make my pages more appealing to search engines.

My intent here is not to dive deeply into the costs and benefits of providing a transcript, but to point out that you will face similar cost-benefit considerations for practically every aspect of your podcast. How many more followers will you attract by excerpting portions of video to share on social media? Is that slick promotional image worth spending an hour on? Your answers may differ from mine, and may evolve, but my advice is to start simple and expand your offerings as you go, rather than to start by providing every possible deliverable and then risk disappointing your audience when you have to pull back on one or more of them. For all of these, consider whether the time, effort, and money you may invest in each deliverable is justified by the benefit you and your audience gain from it.

I saw this play out in my own business when, in early 2022, I made a significant change to my approach to podcast deliverables. I hired an assistant for two hours per episode to edit the interview transcript and captions. In the first few weeks, we spent time working out how best to allocate this time. For example, we decided that rather than having him do a detailed edit of as much of the transcript as he could in the available time and having me finish any remaining work, he would make as thorough an editing pass as possible through the entire episode within the allotted time.

However, as we continued working together, I realized he could contribute more to my podcast specifically, and to The Indy Author as a whole, in a more strategic role. He had great suggestions for how I could make better use of my video and audio content to improve engagement on YouTube and other social media platforms. We found ways to reduce the time he spent on transcript editing and free his time for this more value-added work.

If I tried to cost-justify my investment in this work based strictly on my podcast earnings, I couldn't do it. However, I believe it's worthwhile for two reasons. First, the expanded video content will eventually open opportunities for earnings on other platforms such as YouTube. Second, the time I save on doing the transcript editing and video and audio content creation myself is time I can reallocate to my fiction writing, the most profitable arm of my writing and publishing business.

Captain's Log

You can capture your answers to these questions in the downloadable worksheet available at TheIndyAuthor.com Podcasting for Authors.

What steps will you take to ensure that you will be able to provide high-quality audio to your listeners?

What other deliverables will you provide when you launch your podcast?

What materials will you produce as a normal part of your podcast that will interest your audience, and that you could produce with little to no additional time and effort?

What additional deliverables might you consider adding over time?

More Resources

Joshua Rivers' introductory *Podcasting for Authors Podcast* Episode 102 for valuable considerations related to choosing your podcast title and your cover artwork

The Indy Author Podcast Episode 51 "Podcasting as Content Marketing with Jerri Williams"

CHOOSING YOUR SCHEDULE

What's the best frequency for posting an episode of a podcast? Regularly! And if you're serious about getting traction as a professional podcaster, a weekly schedule is most common and therefore the one that listeners have come to expect. Weekly episodes are frequent enough to keep an audience engaged but not so frequent as to take too much time from your other creative, professional, or personal endeavors.

Which day of the week is best for a new episode to go up? Any day that's not already occupied by a marquee-name podcast in your niche. *The Indy Author Podcast* focuses on the writing craft and the publishing voyage, so I looked at other podcasts addressing those topics—mainly the other podcasts that I listen to—and picked a day that was less crowded with new episode airings.

What time of day is best for a new episode to go up? I load my content to Libsyn, my podcast hosting platform, and YouTube ahead of time and set them to publish at 7am Eastern. That's my time zone and, when I started, the time zone of most of my listeners as well. I figured that 7am was early enough to make it available for morning commutes, but not so early that there would be a long lag time between when it went live and when I completed the couple of steps in the production process that had to be done after the episode aired.

However, one of the great things about podcasting is that you can reach a global audience, with the attendant consideration that you'll never find a time that is optimal for all your listeners. I asked J. Thorn, who has launched more podcasts than anyone I know, for his thoughts about the best time of day for a podcast to go live, and his response was that committing to a regular schedule is far more important than committing to a particular time of day.

Captain's Log

You can capture your answers to these questions in the downloadable worksheet available at TheIndyAuthor.com Podcasting for Authors.

List the top podcasts in your niche and on what day of the week new episodes air. Based on this information, on what day will you post new episodes of your podcast?

CHOOSING YOUR EPISODE
STRUCTURE

The podcasts I enjoy have a regular structure: introductory content, main content, and wrap-up content. Some include personal updates, some do not. Some hosts read comments from listeners, some do not. Some announce giveaway winners at the beginning, some at the end. I appreciate the regularity of each podcast's structure both because I can anticipate the segments that I enjoy the most, and because I can easily skip past those segments that I enjoy less or that are less applicable to me. Providing a consistent experience will **mark you as a professional** and will help you **build your relationship with your listeners**. Having a regular structure for each episode not only benefits your listeners but also **helps you keep your work and your content organized**.

I've provided information from *The Indy Author Podcast* here as one example of podcast structure and content.

Standard Intro

The standard intro **identifies the podcast and host(s)**, gives the podcast's **topic area** in a tagline format, and provides **contact information**. The standard intro for *The Indy Author Podcast* is:

Hi, this is Matty Dalrymple, and welcome to *The Indy Author Podcast*, where we discuss the writing craft, the publishing voyage, and how we can navigate our way to the readers who will love our books.

More resources are available at TheIndyAuthor.com —and that's Indy with a Y—and on Facebook and Twitter at The Indy Author. If you want to learn about my suspense and thriller novels and short stories, go to MattyDalrymple.com—and that's Matty with a Y.

And now, here's today's episode!

If possible, work your podcast's branding into your intro. In line with my nautical metaphors, I always refer to my nonfiction platform as being related to *the writing **craft** and the publishing **voyage***, and I emphasize this with the reference to *navigating* to the readers who will love our work.

Episode-specific Intro

The episode-specific intro provides an **introduction to that episode's topic and the guest**. It should provide a teaser of the episode's content to hook the listener. Here's an example of the intro for Episode 44 "Using Aggregators versus Going Direct with Dale L. Roberts":

Hello, fellow creative voyagers! In this week's episode of *The Indy Author Podcast*, Dale L. Roberts of Self-Publishing with Dale makes his second appearance on the podcast, this time to talk about Using Aggregators versus Going Direct. Dale discusses the pros and cons of using an aggregator such as Draft2Digital or Findaway Voices versus going direct to platforms such as Amazon, Apple, Barnes & Noble, and Kobo. He gives tips on how to assess which approach best meets your business goals, and, if those goals change, describes the considerations if you switch from one approach to the other. Perhaps most importantly, he emphasizes the importance of factoring in not only the financial cost but also the time cost when assessing your options.

I fold a second section into my episode-specific intro—the **patronage request**.

Dale joins an impressive crew of others who have shared their knowledge with listeners of the podcast ...

Steven James, who in Episode 43 "Twelve Sure-fire Ways to Kill the Suspense of Your Novel" discusses the difference between action and tension, how twists do (and don't) work, and the reader's desire to be both surprised and satisfied.

Joshua Tallent, who in Episode 42 "The Importance of Metadata" discusses how authors can optimize their metadata, and when we need to switch our focus from tweaking metadata to producing more content.

Jenna Moreci, who in Episode 41 "How to Write a Convincing Villain" discusses the importance of knowing your villain as well as you know your protagonist.

... and many more.

With a growing backlist of episodes, and an expanding set of resources available at TheIndyAuthor.com, I've set up a Patreon account to solicit your support to continue this work. Patreon enables you to support creators by pledging a regular financial contribution, which you can start and stop as you wish. Your contribution not only lets me know you benefit from these resources but also helps defray the costs of producing the podcast and of maintaining the website.

To learn more about becoming a patron, please head over to patreon.com/TheIndyAuthor, and that's Indy with a Y, or go to TheIndyAuthor.com and click on the Podcast tab.

If you'd like to make an occasional contribution, perhaps to indicate the value that a specific episode provided to you on your creative voyage, scroll to the bottom of any page at TheIndyAuthor.com and click on the Buy Me a Coffee link to make a small contribution via PayPal or Stripe.

Thank you for considering supporting my work at The Indy Author!

The verbiage after "With a growing backlist of episodes" is more-or-less consistent from episode to episode, and it might be more efficient to record this once and use that same recording in each episode, but I take the time to record it fresh each time because I believe that anything I can do to make this request seem less rote will be more likely to result in action by my listeners. On a more tactical level, I want to avoid an audible difference in voice or room tone between the episode-specific verbiage and the standard verbiage.

I only recently started including a **personal update**, which I insert after the patronage request and before the guest interview. I resisted doing a personal update for a long time. It wasn't that I was uncomfortable about the content; my hesitance was because it felt like an unnecessary complication to coordinate the recording of a personal update, which I wanted to do as close to the air date of the episode as possible, along with all the other moving parts. However, as I thought about the podcasts that I enjoy the most, I realized they all include personal updates. Sometimes, even if I'm not interested in a particular episode's main topic, I'll still tune in to the beginning of the episode to hear the personal update.

I've referenced J. Thorn's quote about the intimate connection that a podcast can provide with your audience, and a personal update deepens that connection. As with all the components of your podcast, think through in advance how personal you want it to be—and, if you plan to discuss family or friends, make sure you've gotten their buy-in first.

If I have any upcoming events, appearances, or publications, I include those in the personal update, and mention that listeners can find links to these at MattyDalrymple.com/Events.

I also include a reference to any **recommended resources**, usually but not always affiliate or sponsor products, in the episode-specific intro; see the chapter "Creating Direct Income with Your Podcast" for more information.

Main Content

I start out every interview with:

> Hello, and welcome to *The Indy Author Podcast*! Today my guest is <u>guest name</u>. Hi, <u>first name</u>! How are you doing?

This provides a smooth transition from the episode-specific intro and, delivered in an appropriately upbeat manner, sets a welcoming and energized tone for the conversation.

Since *The Indy Author Podcast* is an interview format, most of the main content is discussion between me and the guest. I prepare a few high-level questions in advance, and provide these to the guest before the recording, but I avoid a slavish march through my bullet points. When interviewing a guest, see where the discussion naturally takes you, venture into other areas as seems appropriate, and discard any questions that don't fit the flow of the conversation.

Be sure to set an expectation with the guest in advance about a target range for the duration of your conversation (for *The Indy Author Podcast*, this is 30-45 minutes), but be aware that guests can easily lose track of time, especially if they are fully engaged in the conversation. If a guest runs long in a recorded interview, you can shorten it as needed during the edit, or perhaps even break it into a multi-part series. If you find the conversation is flagging before you've reached your minimum target duration, you could consider combining a few such brief conversations into one episode, especially if they have a common theme, or could provide that conversation as an extra resource—separate from a regular podcast episode—to your listeners, or to your sponsors. See the chapter "Creating the Episode" for more tactics for conducting a successful interview.

I end each interview with a request that the guest share their contact information with the audience:

Let our listeners and viewers know where they can find out more about you and your work online!

Guests invest an hour or more of their time prepping for and taking part in the interview—the least you can do is give them an opportunity to promote their work.

Episode-specific Wrap-up

The episode-specific wrap-up should **switch the focus from the guest to the listener**. You can encourage engagement by posing a question related to the episode's topic and asking listeners to respond with comments on your website or other central, easily monitored online location.

When choosing the location to which you will direct listeners, consider both the features of the platform and your business goals related to follower engagement. I used to point people to the episode's page at TheIndyAuthor.com, but my website builder doesn't provide a means of allowing responses to specific comments, making it hard to treat these interactions like conversations, and didn't notify me when comments were posted. I started directing commenters to YouTube not only because it addressed these needs but also because I'm working on increasing traffic to my YouTube channel.

You can also use the episode-specific wrap-up to announce any giveaways the guest is offering, and to announce the winners of the last giveaway. (You can further encourage engagement by drawing the giveaway winner from those who have commented on the podcast.) Make the entry process as easy as possible, and mention any limitations, such as geographic limitations if you don't want to go to the time and expense of shipping a print book to another country. Be sure to specify a date by which listeners must enter to win the give-away, and include the year to accommodate people who listen to the episode after the deadline has passed. See the chapter "Creating the Episode" for more information on giveaways.

Patronage Reminder or Alternate Patronage Method

I could use this section, which follows the episode-specific wrap-up, to remind listeners about the Patreon membership, but instead I use it to offer an alternative patronage method: Buy Me a Coffee.

If you got value from this episode and were thinking, "I wish I could buy Matty a cup of coffee," you can do that! Scroll to the bottom of any page at TheIndyAuthor.com and click Buy Me a Coffee to make a small contribution via PayPal or Stripe.

I've found that offering both an **ongoing membership option and an episode-specific option for patronage** attracts support from listeners who might not gravitate to one or the other of these.

Standard Outro

The standard outro should **remind listeners of the name of the podcast, request actions you would like them to take, and reiterate your contact information**. Like the intro, it should reflect any special branding or "livery" you've developed for your podcast. In my case, the reference to "favorable winds and smooth sailing" reemphasizes the nautical metaphor I use in my discussions of the writing craft and the publishing voyage.

Thank you for listening to *The Indy Author Podcast*! To help others find the podcast, please leave a rating and review on your favorite podcast platform and spread the word to your author friends.

You can find out more about me and my books at mattydalrymple.com—that's Matty with a Y—and at TheIndyAuthor.com—and that's Indy with a Y! You can also connect with me on Facebook and Twitter.

Until next time, here's wishing you favorable winds and smooth sailing on your creative voyage!

When deciding what components to include in your podcast, factor in logistical considerations. For example, if you plan to include a segment in which you comment on current events, then you'll need to record that segment as close to the episode's air date as possible, even if you recorded the main content—perhaps a discussion of how to write effective dialogue —weeks if not months earlier. As we discussed in "Choosing Your Deliverables," start with a simple structure and ramp up, rather than starting with a complex structure and having to scale back.

Captain's Log

You can capture your answers to these questions in the downloadable worksheet available at TheIndyAuthor.com Podcasting for Authors.

What will the structure of your episodes be when you start out?

What components might you consider adding over time?

CHOOSING YOUR PERSONA

As we've discussed, the personal connection that audio enables you to establish with your audience is one of podcasting's greatest strengths, and consistency will help sustain that connection over time. There are two considerations that are intrinsic to the persona you will project through your podcast. First, how much personal information will you share? Second, how profane—how clean or explicit—will your delivery be? Establish your approaches to these early and to stick with them throughout your podcast run, since, as we'll discuss in this chapter, mid-course changes will disconcert your listeners and may cause them to turn elsewhere for content.

How Personal?

If you have a solo show, the format will encourage personal revelations and sharing. In an interview format, on the other hand, oversharing within the interview will shift the focus away from the guest, where it belongs. In this case, consider a personal update as a segment separate from the guest interview. I'd recommend putting the personal update before your interview since your fans may want to listen to that segment even if they're not interested in the main topic. It wasn't until 2020 that I introduced a personal update to *The Indy Author Podcast*, but in retrospect I wish I had done this sooner in order to benefit from that deepened personal connection with my listeners.

Consider the relevance of your personal updates to your podcast's topic area, and even to the specific topic of the episode in which that update will appear. My personal updates focus on my own writing craft and publishing voyage, and I believe one benefit of those updates is to demonstrate to my listeners that I have had the same questions, dealt with the same challenges, and experienced the same satisfactions they have as writers.

However, I've also gained unanticipated benefits from sharing information about my work in progress. As part of one of my personal updates, I announced my plan to publish a book on podcasting for authors, and shortly thereafter received an email from Jerri Williams, a retired FBI agent who writes, blogs, and podcasts about FBI cases and the portrayal of the FBI in books, movies, and TV. Jerri is an enthusiastic and expert practitioner of podcasting as content marketing, and she volunteered to come on the podcast and share her expertise with me and my audience. Some great material from that episode made its way into this book, and that's an opportunity I might never have had if I hadn't shared news of my podcasting for authors book as part of a personal update.

No matter how personal your personal updates will be, make sure they are *your* updates, not friends' or family members' (unless they've given you explicit approval to share that information).

Once you've determined at how personal a level you want to share, keep this consistent. My personal updates on *The Indy Author Podcast* are mainly focused on my writing and publishing work; if I were suddenly to share something about my family life or my health, my listeners might be taken aback. Similarly, if I had established a precedent for sharing details of my family life or health, my listeners might be disappointed if I then switched to updates only about my professional work.

How Profane?

It is possible to regroup on many of the decisions you make when you're preparing for your podcasting voyage if you find your original approach isn't supporting your goals. However, one you should choose early and stick with is **whether your podcast will be clean or explicit**, based on its topics and its language. This is not a casual decision—almost any platform to which you load your audio or video will require you to indicate this.

The issues with a mid-course change to the level of profanity in your podcast are obvious if you start family-friendly and then start dropping F-bombs. The parent who's used to listening to your podcast in the car with their small children in the back seat won't be pleased if you take them by surprised with this change in direction. The audio and video platforms will be even less pleased if you fail to change your metadata to indicate that you are taking a less family-friendly tack.

Even a change in the other direction could be tricky. If your audience likes your gritty language or provocative topics and then finds you've cleaned up your act, they may be disappointed and go elsewhere for their podcast (and profanity) fix.

You might consider this in a similar vein as choosing the topic of your podcast—G-rated topics and language will provide you with a wider potential audience but less differentiation, whereas R-rated topics and language will limit your reach but will provide a clear differentiator. Consider, though, that any adult-only output will encourage adult-only input, since the tone of your podcast will set the tone of your listeners' interactions with you. Be sure you'll be comfortable interacting with your listeners in this way.

Captain's Log

You can capture your answers to these questions in the downloadable worksheet available at TheIndyAuthor.com Podcasting for Authors.

Will you provide personal updates on your podcast? If yes, what type of information will you share? What will be off-limits?

Will your podcast be clean or explicit?

If explicit, what are the language and topics you will incorporate that will give it this rating, and what might that mean in terms of the audiences to which you promote your podcast?

CHOOSING YOUR LIVERY (A.K.A. BRANDING)

In the previous chapter, we discussed the persona you want to present to your audience: what level of personal information you plan to share, and in how clean or explicit a manner you plan to present your content. In this chapter, **we'll focus on your physical presentation**.

The world's most successful products have an immediately identifiable brand: the Starbucks' siren, the Apple apple, the Nike swoosh. But as individuals, and especially as creatives, it's sometimes hard to think about how to apply the concept of branding to our own work. Of course, the nautical world provides a metaphor: a ship's livery.

In the cruise ship world, *livery* refers to the design and paint scheme used on the ship's exterior, which often include variations on or references to the company's logos and symbols. For example, Cunard ships are easily recognizable by their black hulls and red funnels, livery that has remained largely unchanged for almost 200 years. A glance across a busy harbor would confirm that you're looking at a Cunard ocean liner, not a Celebrity or Royal Caribbean cruise ship, and the recognizable Cunard livery would telegraph a message about the experience you would expect aboard that ship.

Similarly, the "livery" of your podcast should telegraph the aspect of your podcast that sets it apart from others, and those characteristics will help listeners identify with you as an individual, not merely as an anonymous voice behind the microphone.

Cover Art and Logo

All podcasts have cover art: the square image that appears on podcast players. Open your favorite podcast player and check out the cover art; these images are generally tiny, so visual simplicity is key. When determining the cover art for your own podcast, consider this great advice from Jerri Williams about her redesign of the cover art for her podcast, *FBI Retired Case File Review*:

I redesigned the logo because my podcast logo was not an appropriate podcast logo. Podcasts logos need to be clean. They need to be fresh. You need to be able to look at it in a little tiny box and be able to see exactly what that podcast is about.

In the original cover art I did that on overload. I had a man in handcuffs. I had the FBI seal. I had a gun. I had the word. It was just way too much. People would look at it and say, *You know, you really should clean this up a bit*. But I was afraid ... I really thought if I changed it, then people wouldn't recognize it. And that was just totally untrue.

The new cover art immediately tells you *FBI*. It's very clean. It's very fresh. And I can tell you that I have seen a definite increase in the number of people who are listening to the podcast since that's been out. And it's all because if they're scrolling through and my podcast shows up, what hits them is that gold 'FBI' — *bam*. And I really do believe that just because I changed the logo, instead of losing listeners, I actually am gaining listeners.

JERRI WILLIAMS, *THE INDY AUTHOR PODCAST* EPISODE 51

Podcasters often incorporate their logo in their cover art, as Jerri did. Since I use nautical metaphors to explore the writing craft and the publishing voyage, The Indy Author logo, which I use for my podcasts, incorporates an image of a ship, with a pen forming its stem (as in "from stem to stern"). I use the nautical metaphor more sparingly in my podcast than in my writing, but my goal is that if a listener hears a podcast host equate a well-crafted story to a smoothly sanded and varnished hull, or equate the indy publishing world to a speedboat sharing the waters with the supertanker of traditional publishing, they will say, "Ah, that must be The Indy Author." My logo helps reinforce that. Such overt "livery" is not a requirement for a podcast, or may be something that you develop over time, but it is a method you can use to attract and engage your audience, and to differentiate your podcast from the ocean of others.

Clothing and Accessories

If you're recording and publishing video as well as audio, your choice of your literal livery—your clothing and accessories—can help **support your brand**.

I had two goals when I selected the type of clothing and accessories to wear for the podcast interviews. I wanted a consistent look for my portion of the video to provide visual consistency when video thumbnails display in a format such as a YouTube playlist. I also wanted my look to be understated so that the focus would be on my guest, not on what I was wearing.

I ended up laying in a supply of three-quarter-length-sleeve jewel neck T-shirts in similar blue and green tones. This style is practical because it's comfortable—no fussing with binding or slipping clothes during the recording—and works year 'round. The only jewelry I wear is a simple necklace and earrings—the non-dangling kind because drop earrings hit my earbuds as I move my head and make distracting noises.

Simplifying my clothing and accessories had the added benefit of removing a decision point from my recording prep. Because I put the last shirt I wore at the bottom of the pile, all I have to do is grab the shirt on top of the pile, pick my earrings, and I'm ready to go.

For an especially strong brand tie-in, consider getting shirts made with your podcast's logo, as Dale L. Roberts has done for his YouTube channel videos for *Self-Publishing with Dale*.

Captain's Log

You can capture your answers to these questions in the downloadable worksheet available at TheIndyAuthor.com Podcasting for Authors.

Do you have a brand you want to project, or one you would like to develop?

What livery will you use to do that?

CHOOSING THE TECH

In this chapter, I share the technology I use for *The Indy Author Podcast*, which I believe represents a good balance of quality and cost-effectiveness. I have kept this information high level so that it remains relatively evergreen, but you can find additional details and links at TheIndyAuthor.com Podcasting for Authors.

Computer

I'm an Apple devotee, and I love the balance of portability and power of my MacBook Air. If I need more display real estate than my laptop provides, I connect an auxiliary monitor using a docking connection.

Microphone and Earbuds

Every podcasting expert I have ever heard talk about podcasting technology shares one core piece of advice: don't rely on your computer's built-in microphone. I use a Blue Yeti USB microphone, which is one of the most commonly recommended inexpensive mics for podcasting. Select a microphone with a cardioid pickup pattern so that it's primarily picking up your voice rather than the surrounding room tone.

In addition to a mic like the Blue Yeti, it's a good idea to use (mic-less) earbuds. This will prevent other participants' voices from feeding into your mic and degrading the audio. These are inexpensive, and in-ear models are quite unobtrusive, so there's really no excuse for not using earbuds.

Online Meeting Platform

I use Zoom for The Indy Author Podcast. It's so ubiquitous that almost any guest will be familiar with it, and resources for troubleshooting are easy to find.

Audio and Video Editing and Transcription

For audio and video editing and transcription, I use Descript, and I can't recommend it highly enough. You can load an audio or video file to Descript and it creates a fairly accurate transcript. Furthermore, by editing the transcript, you edit the audio and video: for example, if during the recording of the episode you say, "Excuse me for a minute, my dog just knocked over my microphone," you can edit those words out of the transcript and that section will also be edited out of the audio and video. Descript is an invaluable tool for podcasters like me who don't have experience with traditional audio and video editing tools (and don't have the bandwidth to learn).

Descript also enables you to create audiograms—video snippets that display a sound wave under a display of the words being spoken—which is a handy tool for posting brief snippets of your interview on social media.

Finally, Descript offers an overdub feature which enables

you, after training Descript on your voice, to make corrections to audio by typing in the desired verbiage—for example, correcting "My dog Juno just knocked over my microphone" to "My dog Sophie just knocked over my microphone" just by deleting "Juno" from the transcript and typing in "Sophie."

Podcast Hosting Platform

If you're an indy author, you may be familiar with ebook aggregators like Draft2Digital that allow you to maintain your ebook content in one place and distribute it to many retail platforms. A **podcast hosting platform** provides a similar service for distribution to audience-facing podcast platforms. My podcast host is Libsyn, which in turn distributes it to platforms such as Amazon, Android, Apple, Google Podcasts, Spotify, and Stitcher. In exchange for this service, I pay a small monthly fee.

There are hosting platforms that don't charge for this service, but these are for-profit entities and they need to make their money somewhere. "Somewhere" is often through ad placement, and podcasters may not have control over the ads that listeners will hear before, after, and even during the episodes. The ad may not have any connection to the topic of your podcast, in which case you risk confusing your listeners. Even worse, the ad might be for a product, service, or personality to which you object.

As an indy author, the ability to control my content—and the content that surrounds it—is vitally important to me, so it's well worth the few extra dollars a month I pay to ensure that I have full control over the messages I'm sending out to my listeners.

Captain's Log

You can capture your answers to these questions in the downloadable worksheet available at TheIndyAuthor.com Podcasting for Authors.

What technology will you use for the following components of your podcast, or what additional research do you need to do before making a selection?

- *Computer*
- *Microphone and Earbuds*
- *Online Meeting Platform*
- *Audio and Video Editing and Transcription*
- *Podcast Hosting Platform*

More Resources

TheIndyAuthor.com Podcasting for Authors

PART 4
SETTING SAIL

"It is not the ship so much as the skillful sailing that assures the prosperous voyage."

GEORGE WILLIAM CURTIS

SETTING SAIL - INTRODUCTION

"It's the set of the sails, and not the gales,
  Which determines the way it goes."

ELLA WHEELER WILCOX

In Part 4 - Setting Sail, we'll focus on the ongoing operation of the podcast, and those components that will determine **the professionalism of your product**. This professionalism, I would argue, is the other non-negotiable element of launching a podcast (in addition to high-quality audio, as discussed in the chapter "Choosing Your Deliverables").

"Professional" does not necessarily mean experienced. Professionalism is as important whether you're preparing to record your first episode or your five hundredth. In fact, early in our podcasting voyage, professionalism is a strategy we can deploy to compensate for a lack of experience.

"Professional" also does not imply stodgy. There are

podcasters who are known for their frequent deployment of "the F-bomb" who are nonetheless supremely professional.

Professionalism means creating a plan for your podcast, working diligently on executing that plan, and leaving nothing to chance. It also means **being respectful of your guests' and your listeners' time and attention**—making sure they get as much value from the experience as you do.

Professionalism paves the way for achieving the podcast goals discussed in Part 2 - Determining Your Destination:

- **Establishing connections with guests** - Anyone who agrees to appear on your podcast is making a commitment of their time and energy. In fact, if they're not completely comfortable speaking about themselves or their area of expertise or are nervous about being recorded in audio or video, they're making a personal sacrifice to accommodate your invitation. You owe it to them to extend the professional courtesies of being well prepared, being on time for your recording, being respectful in your interaction with them, and maximizing the value of their time by making the best use of the knowledge they share.

- **Building community with your listeners** - Your listeners are the rationale for everything you do as a podcaster. They are the reason guests will accept your invitations. The value you provide to them drives their willingness to support your income creation goals. They are investing their time and attention in your podcast, and you need to repay that investment with professional-level content.

- **Creating income with your podcast** - If you have a goal of earning money from your podcast, then the value of professionalism is clear. Listeners will be more likely to patronize your podcast through tools like Patreon or Buy Me a Coffee if they see that their money is going to a professional effort. They will be more likely to take advantage of your affiliate links if they have evidence that the products or services you recommend have a professional's assessment behind them. They'll be more likely to follow you from the podcast to other income-creating offerings such as books or courses if they have an expectation based on your podcast that those offerings will be professionally produced. Sponsors will be more likely to sign up to support your podcast if you've demonstrated a professional approach to its production.

Professionalism is *not* something to build over time; **it should be apparent from your very first episode.** Unless you're already a celebrity in the niche in which you'll be podcasting, you'll probably start your podcast with a tiny audience. You can use those first episodes as a "shakedown cruise," during which you can tweak and refine your processes.

However, keep in mind that by the time your fifth (or tenth or fiftieth) episode goes out, you will have attracted fans who will go back and listen to your entire backlist, and you don't want those first episodes to have been produced in an amateurish, slipshod manner. You will certainly improve over time, and the strategies you apply to your podcast will evolve, but make sure you can be as proud listening to that first episode as you are listening to your most recent one. The information in Part 4 - Setting Sail will equip you to do that.

Captain's Log

You can capture your answers to these questions in the downloadable worksheet available at TheIndyAuthor.com Podcasting for Authors.

What does professionalism mean to you, and how will you act on that in your podcast?

LINING UP GUESTS

Except for podcasts that are exclusively solo shows, most podcasts will include guests as a regular feature or as a special event. This chapter will address how to identify possible guests and how to select those that will be the best match for your podcast from that pool.

The first guests will be the hardest to book, since you haven't yet established a presence. For this reason, consider pursuing guests with whom you already have an established relationship. This will have the added benefit that a friendly face on video or a friendly voice on audio will help calm any jitters you may have. Choose people for whom you can buy a beer if you forget to hit the *Record* button until thirty minutes into your conversation. However, keep in mind that knowing the guest personally doesn't mean you can lower the professionalism of your handling of the guest and the episode. **The first guest you book will open up a route to a few more, and the second guest still more, so that your pool of potential guests will expand exponentially over time.**

Let's say your podcast topic is *the writing craft of short fiction*. Perhaps you belong to a critique group and have always admired another member's handling of dialogue. That would be a great guest and topic for an early episode. Perhaps your next invitation goes out to the facilitator of the critique group, to discuss facilitation tips and tricks. That guest might mention another short fiction writer who has been a mentor to him or her —another great candidate for your podcast. At each step, you share the previous episodes with your new invitee to demonstrate your credibility and professionalism. With each episode, you get more comfortable with the podcast process and technology and are continually refining your interviewing skills. Eventually, you build up an episode backlist and a reputation that will provide entrées to the most well-known and successful short fiction authors.

I don't intend the progression I describe to reflect the quality of the guest. The discussion with that fellow critique group member about his or her advice on dialogue might be one of your most engaging (and the discussion with the famous short fiction author might be a dud). Instead, it is to acknowledge the reality that the more well-known your guest, the more sought after they will be and the more challenging it will be to interest them in an appearance on your podcast. As experts in their fields, they will also be accustomed to being interviewed by professionals who have been in the business for years. Give yourself a little time before approaching these potential guests.

Your guests can assist you in this progression to better-known experts. That short fiction mentor will be more likely to accept your invitation if their mentee paves the way through an introduction. In fact, part of my standard wrap-up with my podcast guests after finishing the interview is to ask them for suggestions for other guests who would be a good match for *The Indy Author Podcast*, and to get their permission to use their names when approaching the recommended guest. (Doing this at the end of the recording session means the guest will have experienced the podcast and your interview skill and style, and so will be able to make more informed recommendations.) A well-known guest is likely to recommend other well-known people, and so once you've reached the point of having an opportunity to speak with your most desired guests, you'll easily be able to find more of the same.

This might seem like name-dropping, but it's for a good cause and an unselfish purpose. It saves potential guests from having to do an independent assessment of whether to invest the time to participate in an interview with you. If they see that you've already hosted a guest whose name they recognize and whose reputation they respect, it's easy for them to decide that they should be part of your podcast.

Once you've identified your potential guests, **what considerations should go into whether you will issue an invitation?** Consider how comfortable with and proficient in podcast-type discussion the guest is. There are various ways you can judge this. If a potential guest is a professional speaker, you can be fairly certain that they'll be comfortable speaking in a (virtual) public forum. Seeing them speak, or speaking with them one-on-one, will give you a sense of how smooth their speech is. Lots of "um's" and "you know's" shouldn't necessarily knock someone out of the running as a potential guest, but you'll want to factor in additional editing time.

There's also the hard-to-define consideration of how dynamic and engaging your speaker will be. There are people who could hold you spellbound with a story about nautical knot-tying, and people who could bore you with a description of their round-the-world cruise. You want to find more of the first for (and eliminate more of the second from) your podcast, so always try at least to find an online video or recording of the potential guest so you can get a sense of which they are.

In fact, I've invited a number of guests onto *The Indy Author Podcast* after hearing them on other podcasts. However, I never ask them to address exactly the same topic they addressed on that earlier podcast—my topic is usually focused on a sub-topic they might have mentioned in the earlier interview. I also always acknowledge the earlier podcast and, because my topic is slightly different, encourage my listeners to listen to that episode as well.

As a final note, you should *not* have to pay guests to appear on your podcast. I've interviewed some pretty big names in the writing and publishing worlds, and none of them has ever asked for payment.

Captain's Log

You can capture your answers to these questions in the downloadable worksheet available at TheIndyAuthor.com Podcasting for Authors.

Who are five guests you will invite to the early episodes of your podcast?

To what additional guests might they be able to provide introductions?

PREPARING FOR THE EPISODE

By this point, you've spent a lot of time considering how to prepare for your podcast. In this chapter, we'll examine how to prepare for an episode.

Doing Your Research

You no doubt already know a certain amount about potential guests and their topics before issuing your invitation—otherwise, how would you know whether they'll be a good fit for your podcast? Gauge the amount of research that makes sense for you to do before and after a guest accepts your invitation. Reading the latest books by potential guests will enable you to pose appropriate questions in your invitations and might increase the likelihood that they will accept. Reading their entire backlist will not necessarily be time well spent if they end up declining your invitation.

Once a guest has accepted an invitation, you can plunge into any additional research you want to do to prepare yourself for the interview. Even when you think you have completed your research, periodically check in on your guest and their topic online in the lead-up to your interview. You want to be aware of any late-breaking kudos—for example, if your guest's book was just nominated for an award—since you'll want to mention that in your introduction. You also want to be aware of any less favorable reasons for your guest to hit the news—for example, if he or she has made an ill-informed social media post —since you don't want to ask for their advice on attracting fans on social media without being aware that they've just ignited a firestorm on Twitter. (If the faux pas is egregious enough, you might need to consider withdrawing the invitation.)

Finally, never pretend to have more knowledge about a topic than you do. If your guest mentions a book that you're not familiar with, don't try to fake your way through it. If knowledge of that reference seems important for your discussion, ask your guest to explain—I can guarantee they will be happy to do so.

Scheduling Your Guests

Coordinating the scheduling of the interview with your guest can be tricky. You don't want your first interactions to be this email thread: "What about this date and time?" ... "That doesn't work for me, what about this date and time?" ... "No, I have a conflict, what about ..."

You can use software to avoid this back-and-forth—for example, Calendly or YouCanBook.Me. You identify available time slots, and guests can then search for one that works for them. I've used these apps as a guest on other podcasts and they work well.

Although I wouldn't discount using one of these apps in the future, I haven't done it yet because I want more control over the scheduling of my interviews. For example, if I'm scheduling two interviews that won't be as mentally taxing for me (for example, on topics with which I'm familiar), I might be willing to schedule both for the same day. However, if I'm scheduling two interviews that are going to require more mental energy, then I'd want the option of scheduling those on different days.

I've found that if I can be sufficiently clear and thorough in my communications, scheduling via email works fairly well, especially if I know the guest's time zone. I provide enough options—weekdays and weekends, morning and afternoon, and so on—that guests can usually find one that works for them with no back-and-forth. Just make sure you don't have too many of these emails in play at once; otherwise you risk having two guests choose the same time slot.

Confirming and Prepping Guests

Once a guest has agreed to an interview and you have mutually agreed on a time for the recording or live event, send them an invitation with the details and separately send them an email confirming the arrangements for the recording, topics to be covered, and logistics. (I recommend sending the invite and the email separately because I find that meeting invites tend to go missing more often than emails.) Below is a sample confirmation email.

Subject: The Indy Author Podcast Prep - Michael La Ronn

Michael, thank you for agreeing to be a guest on The Indy Author Podcast! I have provided some details for you below--I'm looking forward to our chat.

Logistics

The interview is scheduled for Monday, January 1 at 10am Eastern (include the guest's timezone if different) via Zoom, recording both audio for the podcast and video for YouTube. I have sent you an invitation with the information for the meeting and have also provided the information below.

(Provide online meeting link, password, etc.)

We'll have a chance to chat a bit and get settled before I start recording.

We will aim for 30-45 minutes. Click here for some tips for our conversation and recording.

Please send me a brief bio, a headshot, and the website and social media links that you'd like me to use for the show notes and for posting promotions for the episode.

In the week following the airing of your episode, I will be promoting it on social media (links below) and in my weekly email newsletter; if you have not yet subscribed to my newsletter and would like to do so, please click here.

If you need to reschedule the interview, it's generally not a problem--please just let me know by the previous day.

Topic: Estate Planning for Authors

- Planning your estate
- Organizing your estate
- Managing your estate
- Sharing confidential information with your heirs
- Guarding against scams

Best,

Matty

Include your own website and social media links so that the guest can easily learn more about you.

Here are the tips to which I direct guests of the podcast:

To prospective guests of The Indy Author Podcast, thank you for setting aside time to talk with me! Here is some information to ensure that our conversation is a great experience for us and for your fans and followers, current and future!

Unless otherwise arranged, all episodes are recorded via Zoom, and I will post both audio and video. I will edit the conversation, so no problem if you are beset by a case of the hiccups.

We will aim for 30-45 minutes for our chat.

The listeners of the podcast are writers and authors, published and unpublished, indy and traditional, so discussion should focus on topics related to the writing craft and the publishing voyage.

Find a quiet space where you won't be disturbed by people or pets.

Turn off your phone and silence notifications on your computer.

Don't rely on the built-in microphone on your computer; even inexpensive mic-equipped earbuds will provide better sound quality.

Since I will be posting video of our conversation, check what the camera will pick up, and adjust accordingly.

Think of this as a chat over coffee.

Once the episode is up, please share it with your friends, fans, and followers!

Questions in Advance?

As illustrated in the sample confirmation email above, I always provide guests with a few broad questions or topics to ensure that we're on the same page in terms of the focus of the conversation. I often capture more detailed questions in my own notes. If the guest is experienced with the interview format, and seems comfortable as we talk, then I may range into these and other questions depending on where the conversation takes us. However, if the person isn't experienced or seems nervous, then I'll generally stick to the questions I've sent them. As noted in the chapter "Choosing Your Mode, Medium, and Venue," a benefit of a recorded interview over a live interview is the ability to edit out any situations where the guest (or you) gets flustered.

Captain's Log

You can capture your answers to these questions in the downloadable worksheet available at TheIndyAuthor.com Podcasting for Authors.

Having one of your target guests in mind, what research will you do before you approach them about being on your podcast?

If they accept, what additional research will you do before the interview?

More Resources

TheIndyAuthor.com Podcasting for Authors

TheIndyAuthor.com Podcast For Guests of The Indy Author Podcast

CREATING THE ENVIRONMENT

Webb Chiles is credited with saying, "A sailor is an artist whose medium is the wind." We might say that a podcaster is an artist whose medium is sound.

You may choose to provide both audio and video of your podcast episodes, but a podcast is primarily an audio product and, as discussed in the chapter "Choosing Your Deliverables," technically high-quality audio is one of the non-negotiable deliverables of a professional podcaster. At base, there are two audio components at play—the sound of the voices, which we'll examine in more detail in the next chapter, "Refining Your Audio and Video Presence," and the sound of the space in which you will be recording, which we'll discuss in this chapter.

Most importantly, find a quiet room. Think about what might cause noise in your environment and what you can do to avoid or minimize it. As someone with three dogs who lives in a neighborhood with a lot of deer, when I'm recording, I put the dogs in a room where they can't see into the backyard.

The ideal recording environment should also be "dry" (from an audio perspective). That means one that is free of hard surfaces, which is why so many podcasters and audiobook narrators record in walk-in closets (and sometimes non-walk-in closets). It's possible to install sound-absorbing wall covering that will make an area conducive to audio recording, and in fact you can purchase audio recording booths to assemble in a basement or unused room, but these not only are expensive but also mean you can't easily use that space for other purposes. A clever idea from audiobook narrator Derek Doepker is to drape blankets over a patio umbrella (deployed indoors, of course), which you can put away when not in use. All these ideas work best if you aren't recording video, unless you have a way to keep your racks of clothes, sound baffles, or blanket-draped umbrella from being your backdrop.

I record *The Indy Author Podcast* in my home office, and the set-up is such that I can block any hard services during recording but can easily disassemble the set-up for non-recording uses. I have a pair of seagrass room dividers, which I set up around my desk, and I drape a dresser which is next to my desk with a blanket. Of course, I close the door to the office. I also use a rolled-up throw rug to block the gap at the bottom of the door to muffle any dog barks. The one hard surface in my recording space that I don't block is the window, because I've prioritized the benefit of getting additional natural light over the small improvement in sound quality that closing the curtains might produce.

You should record all the segments of your podcast—intro and outro material and main content—in the same space, treated in the same way, so that there aren't distracting changes in room tone from one segment to the next.

If you're recording video, then you need to balance excellent audio quality with an attractive background. Video cameras often capture a wider area than one would expect, so make sure that there's nothing in your background that you don't want viewers to see. If you're using a bookcase as a background—a popular choice among authors—make sure the books on view align with the persona you want to project.

A well-chosen background can support your brand livery. For example, I've used variations of nautically-themed decor, such as nautical maps or a picture featuring a body of water, as my background for *The Indy Author Podcast*.

Because I want a different look for video where I'm the guest rather than the host, I've set up my office so that I can sit on the other side of the desk, with a more casual backdrop of a cushioned chair and curtains. (The curtains actually block an open doorway, but a viewer wouldn't know that there isn't a window behind the curtains unless they read this book.) I place lamps in the background to provide some visual interest but position them in such a way that the unshaded light isn't in line of sight of the camera. Otherwise, the camera automatically adjusts to the brighter background light, which leaves my face in shadow. I reposition the seagrass room dividers to block a dresser, which would give the room an unprofessional bedroomy look.

Captain's Log

You can capture your answers to these questions in the downloadable worksheet available at TheIndyAuthor.com Podcasting for Authors.

What steps can you take to make the environment where you will record your podcasts as conducive to high-quality audio as possible?

What sounds exist in the environment that might need remediation?

If you will be recording video, what do you want in your background to support the persona you want to project?

What do you want to make sure does not appear in the background?

More Resources

The Creative Penn Podcast, Audiobook Narration, Production And Marketing Tips with Joanna Penn and Derek Doepker

REFINING YOUR AUDIO AND VIDEO PRESENCE

We considered podcasting technology in "Choosing the Tech," but there is another tool of the podcasting trade to consider, and that is our voice. If you're recording video as well as audio, you need to consider your appearance on camera. In this chapter, I share some of the lessons I've learned along the way about getting comfortable with and optimizing your personal audio and video presence.

Audio

"I really like the way I sound on a recording" said no one ever, and **self-consciousness about or even active dislike of our voice** can stand in the way of pursuing a podcast. Dissatisfaction with our recorded voice can be driven by a few considerations.

One source of self-consciousness is **expectations versus reality** ... the fact that our voice in a recording sounds different from the voice we hear in our head. Here's an explanation from the BBC:

What makes a recording of our voice sound so different... and awful? It's because when you speak you hear your own voice in two different ways. ... The first is through vibrating sound waves hitting your ear drum, the way other people hear your voice. The second way is through vibrations inside your skull set off by your vocal cords. Those vibrations travel up through your bony skull and again set the ear drum vibrating. However as they travel through the bone they spread out and lower in pitch, giving you a false sense of bass. Then when you hear a recording of your voice, it sounds distinctly higher.

The issue is less the actual pitch of your voice than the disconnect between what you're used to hearing inside your head and what you hear in a recording. Sometimes just understanding the science behind the difference can help alleviate this concern. The practice of hearing your recorded voice, as you will inevitably do as a normal part of the podcast production process, will also help. Like pretty much everyone else, I didn't like the sound of my voice when I started podcasting, but after having listened to my recorded voice a lot, I've adjusted my expectations and it no longer bothers me.

Another source of self-consciousness can be **verbal tics**, like saying "kind of" or "you know" as filler phrases or repeating a word over and over until your brain catches up with your mouth. My own downfall, at least during podcast recordings, is starting every sentence with "So ..."

Choosing a recorded rather than live format can greatly help with this, since you can edit out these verbal tics. In fact, Descript, the software I use to edit the audio and video of my podcast, has an automated filler word detection and removal feature (which on its own is worth the monthly fee). Another great feature Descript offers is automated shortening of pauses.

If you're using a live format, being aware of these tics can help, but being too focused on them can actually exacerbate the issue. Try to replace verbalized tics with silence, but don't obsess over it. In podcasts that are not heavily edited, you will hear plenty of such imperfections from hosts whose speech is perfectly pleasant to listen to.

A third possible source of self-consciousness is an actual **speech impediment**. I have a slight lisp that I only notice if I listen to myself on a recording. If you find yourself in a similar situation, you could pursue speech therapy to overcome the impediment, but before you take any drastic action, let's consider some informal market research.

I polled a podcasting mastermind group about how concerned a potential podcaster should be about something like a slight lisp. Many in the group weighed in and, without exception, they said that this consideration should not stand in the way of pursuing a podcast. In fact, many of them called out examples of people with fairly significant speech impediments who have successful podcasts based on the quality of the content, not the radio announcer-like perfection of their voices.

If you're still uncertain, you could do a little market research of your own about others' reaction to your voice. To make the research valid, you can't ask people you know to weigh in—you need to solicit input from strangers, and ideally from people who don't know whose voice they are assessing. Finding such a group can be tricky. Theoretically you could post a brief recording in a podcast-oriented group on social media or on a platform such as SoundCloud and solicit comments, but then the concern is the opposite of asking friends—people in those forums can be all too willing to share negative feedback, and not in a helpful way.

My advice is to **select a few friends who are podcast listeners, then ask them to share the recording with a few of their podcast-listening friends**. A pool of three friends, each sharing with three more people, will give you an input pool that is perfectly sufficient for our needs. Ask your friends to ask their survey pool, *Would you be comfortable listening to this voice in a podcast?* Provide a sense of how much talking you'll be doing in an episode. In an hour-long interview episode, your total talk time might be less than a dozen minutes. In an hour-long solo show, your talk time will be an hour.

When you receive the input, don't just tally the numbers and act on the winning vote. Consider that input along with all the other factors that go into making a successful podcast and make a decision based on a holistic assessment.

If you're still feeling squeamish about your voice, you should not only listen to recordings of your own voice in order to become more comfortable with its sound, but also listen to the podcasters whose shows you enjoy. Rarely do they have those perfect, radio announcer-like voices. They draw in their listeners not based on the beauty of the sounds they produce, but by their expertise or engagement in the topic at hand, by a welcoming demeanor, and by professional-level content. Focus on these aspects and keep your podcasting persona in mind— you will attract listeners with the value you provide and the style in which you provide it.

Video

If you are going to offer video as well as audio of your podcast episodes, then you'll need to come to terms not only with how you sound but also with how you look. In this section, I share some tips that will make your on-camera experience a little more relaxing.

Consider that, for the most common framing for video interviews, you only need to look professional from about mid-torso up.

For make-up wearers, today's high-resolution cameras mean that less is better. The only cosmetic I add to my already minimalist makeup regime is a bit of powder to take the shine off my nose.

Simpler is also better—don't wear jewelry that might jangle or clink when you move, or a hairstyle that will require you to flip your hair out of your eyes periodically (unless that's part of your brand).

In general, for an interview format, visual understatement is the goal, because you want the focus to be on your guest, not on you. And a more understated look can sometimes help address some self-consciousness about appearance.

Just as you need to be willing to review your podcast audio with an ear out for opportunities to improve the experience for your listeners, you need to review your video with an eye out for opportunities to improve the experience for your viewers. For example, I realized that my natural posture when paying close attention to someone was to sit forward and cock my head. On video, however, this doesn't look attentive—it looks combative. Sitting up straight and even leaning back a bit gave me a better visual presentation.

Captain's Log

You can capture your answers to these questions in the downloadable worksheet available at TheIndyAuthor.com Podcasting for Authors.

Do you have experience listening to yourself in audio recordings or watching yourself on video? (If no, create some recordings in the medium you plan to use for your podcast and review them.)

Are there any actions you want to take to address any self-consciousness about your audio or video presence that will remove it as a barrier to starting your own podcast?

CREATING THE EPISODE

All your course plotting—determining your destination and preparing for your voyage—will pay off as you launch into the crux of your podcasting journey: creating the episode. This chapter focuses primarily on an interview format, but much of this advice will smooth the waters of other formats as well.

There are a number of steps you should take as part of every episode or interview recording to ensure that it's the best experience possible for you, any co-hosts, your guests, and your listeners. I could strain for a nautical metaphor, but an aviation analogy works much better.

Pre-flight Checklist

I have a pre-flight checklist I run through before every recording:

- **Reboot computer** - This ensures your computer's processing power isn't being degraded by unused applications or behind-the-scenes processes that build up over time. Do this far enough in advance so that if your computer decides that today's the day to install a major update (as mine did minutes before I was scheduled to start an interview with a well-known thriller writer), it has time to complete before your scheduled recording time.

- **Put the dogs in a room where they can't see outside** - This lowers the possibility of an outburst of barking during the recording.
- **Put a "temporarily out of service" sign** on the door of the bathroom that's on the other side of the wall from where I record my interviews - This ensures no one runs the shower or flushes the toilet while I'm recording.
- **Select the correct microphone** - There's nothing more annoying than connecting a nice podcasting microphone and then realizing later that the audio was recorded on your computer's built-in mic.
- **Put in earbuds** - This ensures that my mic doesn't pick up my guest's audio.
- **Turn off notifications** on the computer - I also close Facebook and Outlook because these seem to consider themselves exempt from the do not disturb setting.
- **Silence phone** (or, if possible, leave it in a different room).

The "Passenger Safety Briefing"

Once the guest has joined my Zoom meeting, but before I hit record, I have a few more "pre-flight" items to review.

- If you don't see your guest using an **external mic or earbuds**, ask them if they have those available. (You will have requested that in your prep material, but not all guests will have noticed or remember.) If they are using an external mic, ask them to confirm that they have it selected.

- Assess the **audio** and make any further suggestions that will improve the audio quality, such as asking them to close the door to the room they're in if you can hear background noise.

- If you're recording **video**, scan their video feed for any easy adjustments they can make to improve the visuals. For example, you might ask them to close the blinds on a window that's creating a glare or to shift the angle of the camera to move a bright lamp out of the shot. This will help the camera auto-adjust to their face rather than to their background. Also scan their environment for any items they may not realize are appearing within camera range, such as open doors or overflowing laundry hampers.

- Ask them to **turn off notifications** on their computer and silence their phone.

- Review any **questions you have highlighted in your interview notes**, such as confirming the correct pronunciation of their name (although it's courteous to try to find out online so you have some idea) and whether they prefer to have you use their full first name or a nickname.

- Ask the guest **if they have any questions** before you start the interview.

Finally, don't tell the guest, "Don't be nervous!" unless that is followed with an actual reason they shouldn't be nervous (for example, "I heard you speak at a conference and loved your take on this topic" or "this is recorded, so don't be concerned if you need to take a break—I can edit that out"). If they're already nervous, telling them not to be nervous is just going to make them more nervous ... and maybe irritated with you. If they are *not* already nervous, enough admonitions not to be nervous will make them so. If they seem nervous, you're more likely to calm their nerves with some casual chat before hitting record.

"In-flight Entertainment"

You want your interaction with your guest to be a conversation, not a structured march through a set of pre-prepared questions. Don't just mark time until you get to ask your next question; listen to what he or she is saying. A guest's response to a question might lead naturally in a slightly different direction than you had anticipated. If that direction is in line with the general topic of the interview, and if you feel the guest will be open to it, follow that path. This approach is easier in a recorded interview than in a live interview, since if recorded, you can edit out any pauses you need to collect your thoughts for the next portion of the conversation.

For interview format episodes, keep the attention on the guest. Don't use the show as an excuse to interject information about you and your work at every opportunity. If talking about your own work is important to you, consider doing this using a solo format—or the occasional solo episode—rather than an interview format.

After Landing

Once you've stopped recording, there are a few follow-up items to discuss with your guest.

Let them know what the **anticipated air date or timeframe** is for their episode, while also acknowledging that circumstances might require a change of schedule. Assure them that you'll let them know when the episode airs.

If you want to offer **giveaways** as part of your podcast, ask guests if they'd like to offer one. Giveaways can be helpful in encouraging engagement with listeners and viewers if you draw the winner name from among those who leave a comment on the episode. Ideally, the giveaway should align with your topic— for example, for *The Indy Author Podcast*, a book on the writing craft or the publishing voyage. By waiting until after your conversation with the guest to ask them about a giveaway, not only have you built up goodwill (assuming your conversation went well), but you and your guest will have a better idea of what offering would be a good match for the theme of the episode. For example, if my podcast guest is a fiction author, I might steer them toward offering a novel that demonstrates a concept discussed in the episode.

If the guest has ebooks available on a platform like Book-Funnel, that can be a fairly painless way to deliver the giveaway to the winner. If the guest is willing to provide a print copy, sourcing it from a platform like Bookshop.org, which benefits indy bookstores, will build more goodwill among your listeners than sourcing it from Amazon. A signed print copy will be an extra-special reward for a lucky fan.

Regardless of the form the giveaway takes, make sure the guest knows you will select the winner and get his or her contact information, but the guest is responsible for delivering the give-away to the winner.

(I have actually eliminated giveaways for my own podcast because I found that, even with the guest being responsible for fulfillment, the benefits in terms of listener and viewer engagement weren't worth even the usually small amount of time I spent coordinating the giveaways.)

Finally, ask guests if they have **ideas for other guests or topics**. Asking this after you've completed your conversation will mean they have a better sense of the focus of your podcast and of your style as a host, and can refine their recommendations accordingly. If you believe that an online introduction will be helpful, ask the guest if they'll be willing to provide this. (Ask them to hold any introductions until you are ready to issue your invitation to the proposed guest.)

Captain's Log

You can capture your answers to these questions in the downloadable worksheet available at TheIndyAuthor.com Podcasting for Authors.

What might you want to change or add in your own flight checklist?

What is one thing you want to be sure to keep in mind during your interactions with your guests (for example, Keep the focus on the guest)? *(You can jot this on a sticky note and attach it to your monitor as a reminder during the live event or recording.)*

MAKING THE MOST OF YOUR CONTENT

One of the most important pieces of advice I have to share about podcasting—and, in fact, about any effort that results in the creation of content—is **not to shortchange yourself in terms of the work to which you can put this content**. Let's turn to another nautical metaphor.

Consider all the steps involved in building a beautiful cedar strip canoe: cutting and attaching the forms, cutting and milling the strips, laminating and attaching the stems, stripping the hull, planing and sanding (and sanding and sanding) and varnishing the hull. You'd never invest all that labor—all that sweat, tears, and possibly blood—take the canoe out for a paddle, then relegate it to its rack, never to be used again. You'd be sure to use it at every opportunity.

The same holds true of the content you create as part of your podcast, a labor of sweat and possibly tears (although we hope not blood). Once you have gone to all the work of producing a podcast episode—lining up a guest or topic, doing the needed research, recording the episode, editing the audio and video, posting it on your podcasting hosting platform—your work is not finished ... but then neither is the benefit you can gain from it.

Enlisting Your Guest's Promotional Support

When an episode airs, notify your guest of its availability and make it easy for them to share it with their social media followers by providing the podcast's URL as well as a link that has been shortened using a tool such as Bitly. These links should point them to a resource, such as a page on your website, that contains additional information: transcript, show notes, and links to the podcast on various platforms.

Here's the template I use for my podcast episodes:

Your episode of *The Indy Author Podcast* is up!

Full URL: link

Shortened URL: link

YouTube URL: link

Over the coming week, I will be promoting it on social media—The Indy Author on Facebook and Twitter and (if appropriate) Matty Dalrymple on Facebook and Twitter.

I will also be promoting it to my email newsletter list; if you are not yet subscribed and would like to do so, please click here.

I'd love any support you can provide in promoting The Indy Author Podcast (on Amazon Music, Android, Apple, Google Podcasts, Libsyn, Spotify, Stitcher, and YouTube) to your author friends and fans. I would also love it if you would rate and review the podcast on your favorite podcast platform.

Thank you so much for taking the time to be a guest
on *The Indy Author Podcast*!

_____

If you book a guest that has an assistant or publicist, include them on this email. Those people may be even more active in sharing and promoting the episode than the guest will be.

The easier you make it for your guest and their associates to access information about the episode, the more likely they are to promote it.

Promoting Every Episode

As you're editing the episode, keep an eye out for **bite-sized bits of content** you can use to entice people to listen to the entire episode: passages that are especially intriguing or are a good representation of the episode's topic. I clip these out as video excerpts.

Daily during the week following an episode airing, I **post these excerpts** on social media. I flag my guests' accounts—for example, @selfpubwithdale—to make sure they see these posts. Guests often share these out to their own fans and followers, thereby expanding the podcast's reach and ideally drawing in more listeners. Posting these excerpts daily for the week following the airing aligns nicely with the standard wisdom that a person has to see a message seven times before it begins to sink in. By the end of the week, the social media followers of my guests will have The Indy Author much more deeply embedded in their consciousness than if I limited my outreach to one communication when the episode first aired.

When the week of episode promotion is complete, I'm ready

with the next episode, meaning that those who are following me on Facebook or Twitter are getting a useful piece of content daily. I also include links to the episodes in my weekly email newsletter.

Repurposing Content

Even at the end of a week focused on promotion of the most recent episode, there are still more opportunities to use this content to continue to produce value for your audience, your guests, and you.

Keep an eye out for opportunities to **refer to material in previous episodes**. Does a guest mention a tip for creating multi-dimensional characters that reminds you of a conversation you had in an earlier episode about creating a compelling villain? If you realize it in the moment, mention it during the discussion. If you realize it after the recording is complete, include a reference in the show notes. In either case, include a link to enable people to find that other content easily—content they may have missed in its original form.

This re-use of content not only is efficient for you but also will earn you the appreciation of your guests. After all, they have invested time and effort in the episode and have just as much incentive as you do to make sure the content is shared widely.

Here's a comment from Dale L. Roberts of *Self-Publishing with Dale* after I interviewed him in Episode 34 "Connecting through Video":

> I hopped onto a video chat and hit it off with Matty from the get-go. We easily burned through an hour of content and could've done another hour if time permit-

ted. But just when I thought she was done and it was over, she blew me away. Matty is a promotional machine! Wow!

Matty broke down the interview into small sound bites and broadcast it across social media. I've never been on a podcast where the host has done so much to promote an appearance. I felt like I was slacking with my promotions when looking at her. And you KNOW how heavily I promote my interview appearances.

The opportunity for repurposing your content is greater if that content is evergreen rather than time-specific, such as topics related to news events or to rapidly changing technology. If your content isn't time-bound, put a reminder on your calendar periodically to **check through backlist episodes** for evergreen content that can still provide value to your audience.

As you may have noticed, in this book, I am following my advice by referencing and linking to applicable episodes from *The Indy Author Podcast*. I not only believe that these are valuable examples of the various topics covered in this book, but also want to encourage readers to check out those episodes, learn more about me and my guests, and gain value from the topics covered and the knowledge shared.

Sharing the Love

Keep an eye out for situations where content might interest a particular person or group. For example, when an episode includes content that I believe would be of particular interest to crime writers, I send a notice about its availability to the members of my local Sisters in Crime chapter. (Since a number of my guests have been Sisters in Crime members, I always notify fellow members of those episodes as well.)

If you or your guest gives a shout-out or kudos to another person, let that person know. In Episode 29 of *The Indy Author Podcast*, Zach Bohannon recommended listeners watch Bailey Parnell's TED Talk "Is Social Media Hurting Your Mental Health?" I sent Ms. Parnell a link to the episode, and she responded to me and Zach with a gracious note of thanks. Even if exposure of that episode's content to just one additional person was the only result of that communication, I have the satisfaction of having let a fellow creator know that her material was appreciated and shared. On Episode 43 of *The Indy Author Podcast*, author Steven James told a charming story about Robert Dugoni's daughter, and I dropped Robert a message to let him know. That exchange resulted in Robert agreeing to be a guest on the podcast in Episode 47.

Captain's Log

You can capture your answers to these questions in the downloadable worksheet available at TheIndyAuthor.com Podcasting for Authors.

Based on how evergreen or time-bound your podcast content will be, over how long a time will you be able to continue to share that content so that you, your guests, and your audience get full value from it?

MAKING IT INTERACTIVE

As your podcast following grows, you and your audience will gain the most benefit if you think of the relationship not as a one-way dissemination of information, but as a dynamic interaction.

Consider how disappointing it would be to put out an episode and get no feedback. It's equally disappointing for a listener to post a comment and have it sit unanswered in the comments queue. Making a commitment to keep that relationship with your listeners interactive is the best way to build a true community. In *The Indy Author Podcast* Episode 21, J. Thorn says that failing to reply to listener comments is "the number one cardinal sin." J. says:

I reply to every single comment that shows up on the podcast. I think that's critically important. If you don't engage on your own show, that's a problem.

Considering how many podcasts J. has going at any one

time, and considering how many super-engaged listeners he has, if he can commit to responding to every comment (and as a commenter, I know he does), then we should be able to step up to that commitment as well.

That's not to say that you need to respond exhaustively to every comment. Your response might be, "Joe, thanks for sharing your insight!" Even that simple acknowledgement will encourage further interaction. To make this manageable, make it clear to your listeners what your primary interaction platform will be. For me it is The Indy Author YouTube channel (which, unlike my website, enables commenters to reply to specific comments and notifies me of new comments). This relieves you of the need to monitor all the various outlets on which your podcast appears.

You can also build your relationship with your audience by engaging them in your creative work beyond your podcast. For example, Jerri Williams solicits listeners of her *FBI Retired Case File Review* podcast to become members of her Reader Team. These listeners receive her "FBI Reading Resource," a list of books about the FBI authored by Jerri and, for an excellent podcast tie-in, by the retired FBI agents who have been guests on her podcast. An even more exclusive Advance Reader Team receives advance copies of Jerri's books, meaning that she can count on a couple dozen reviews within a day or two of a book's publication.

The ultimate goal is to build your community to an extent that it is not just a one-way push of information from you to your audience, and not even just a two-way interaction between you and individual listeners, but interactions among multiple listeners—one person commenting on another's post, listeners exchanging ideas about the question at hand or about the episode content in general. At this point, you can become the moderator of the interactions rather than their primary driver.

Captain's Log

You can capture your answers to these questions in the down-loadable worksheet available at TheIndyAuthor.com Podcasting for Authors.

On what platforms (for example, social media, your website, YouTube) will you interact with your audience?

Can you commit to replying to every comment your listeners post?

More Resources

The Indy Author Podcast Episode 34 "Connecting through Video with Dale L. Roberts"

The Indy Author Podcast Episode 51 "Podcasting as Content Marketing with Jerri Williams"

Links to the following resources are available at TheIndy-Author.com Podcasting for Authors:

9 Things Career Authors Don't Do: Podcasting by J. Thorn

REDUCING FRICTION (IMPROVING YOUR PRODUCTION PROCESS)

As an inveterate tinkerer, I love this quote from *Sail Magazine*:

"Every boat, no matter how big or small, is the sum of its parts, and even on the smallest boat there are plenty of parts. ... Any piece of sailing hardware that is not perfect for the job, not well maintained and not perfectly aligned for its task, could be creating friction. Because friction makes you work harder and harms your boat's performance, it pays to take a long, hard look around your boat to see where and how you can make it function as smoothly as possible."

As with boats, we need to ensure that the parts of our podcast are functioning as smoothly as possible. As with sailors, we don't want to work any harder than we need to or lose any performance to an inefficient process. We need to:

- **Understand the process** in order to know

what steps are involved in the production of our podcast,

- **Capture the process** in order to make the steps repeatable,
- **Remove the friction** in order to make the steps manageable, and
- **Assess the cost and benefit** in order to ensure that the benefits of our work continue to outweigh the costs.

Understanding the Process

In 2018, Todd Cochrane, CEO of podcast hosting company Blubrry, reported that 75% of podcasts are no longer in production; in 2019, about 27,000 podcasts stopped releasing new episodes. Many of these experienced "podfade"—when a podcast stops airing new episodes without an announcement or wrap-up.

At one point, *The Indy Author Podcast* might have joined that number. I estimate that at one time I spent as much as ten hours of prep and production time—and sometimes more—for every hour of podcast I put out. I have refined my processes so that the time commitment now is much less (more on that below), but it's still significant. Some of the work encompassed in that time was:

- Identifying a topic and then searching for an appropriate guest ... or identifying a guest and then searching for an appropriate topic
- Scheduling the interview and providing the appropriate prep materials
- Preparing for the recording (researching the topic,

reading or at least reviewing the content of a guest's books, articles, or blogs, etc.)

- Conducting the interview (probably the least time-consuming of all the steps)
- Creating the metadata for the episode (episode description, guest photo, keywords, hashtags)
- Editing the audio, video, and transcript (despite use of the wonderful Descript application, by far the most time-consuming portion)
- Recording the episode-specific intro and outro
- Posting the episode on the hosting platform, TheIndyAuthor.com, YouTube, and my Patreon page
- Posting promotions on Facebook, Twitter, and my email newsletter
- Notifying the guest and any other potentially interested parties (such as people the guest might have mentioned in the interview) of the availability of the episode
- Creating daily promotional posts on Facebook, Twitter, and YouTube in the week following the episode's airing
- Conducting administrative clean-up (for example, deleting earlier versions or clips I hadn't used)

Just typing that list makes me tired.

However, I got past the seven-episode milestone and have no plans to podfade, largely because I'm continuously finding ways of making the process more streamlined while maintaining a positive experience for my guests and my audience.

Capturing the Process

I have created a spreadsheet in which I have captured over 100 steps of the process of producing an episode. The checklist is that long because it's very granular (for example, "Enter tags and keywords on Libsyn"). I made the list that granular not only because I didn't want to forget a step, but also because my goal was to turn some of that work over to another person.

In fact, I have turned a number of those steps over to my podcast assistant, and we have created similarly detailed documentation of our joint processes and continue to refine and streamline them.

Capturing the process as a spreadsheet template means I am also capturing all the episode-specific information that I will need to use repeatedly—episode description, guest bio, keywords and tags, full website URL and shortened URL, etc.—in one easily accessible location.

Removing the Friction

I keep all the data for an episode in one spreadsheet, one tab per episode, so I have easy access to previous episodes' data. As I work through the task list for each episode, I keep an eye out for opportunities for improvement and adjust the spreadsheet accordingly. For example, I reordered some tasks so that I could start a video export from Descript and then have other tasks to work on until the export completed.

When I'm ready to work on the next episode, I copy the tab for the last episode so that I carry forward the improvements I've made. I keep all the information that's applicable across episodes—for example, the task list—in one column and all the information that is episode-specific—for example, an episode's

URL—in another column so that I can easily delete the episode-specific information from the copied sheet for the new episode.

Assessing the Costs and Benefits

Each time I work through an episode, I keep an eye out for steps or tasks that aren't pulling their weight. For example, I used to ask guests if they wanted to provide a giveaway, the winner to be drawn from listeners and viewers who commented on that episode. My goal was to encourage interaction with the podcast's followers, but any small improvement in engagement didn't merit the time I spent coordinating the giveaways, so I discontinued those.

As your episode backlist builds up—as you pass that infamous seven episode milestone—you need to think through the costs (time, money, effort, stress) of the podcast against the benefits you are enjoying, or expect to enjoy (for example, establishing connections with guests, building community with your listeners, creating income). Early on, you may need to rely more on the benefits you expect to enjoy than on the benefits you are currently enjoying to maintain your motivation. The first episode will be the most difficult to create and be the one that will provide you with the least immediate benefit. However, recognizing that podcasting is a long tail game will help you persevere in your podcasting voyage even during those most challenging early days.

Captain's Log

You can capture your answers to these questions in the downloadable worksheet available at TheIndyAuthor.com Podcasting for Authors.

What mechanisms (for example, checklists, templates, etc.)

will you use to help reduce the effort to create the podcast while still keeping the quality of the product high?

How long do you think it will take for the benefits you are enjoying from your podcast to begin to outweigh the cost of the time, money, effort, and stress of its production?

BEING A PODCAST GUEST

Most of this book focuses on your role as a podcast host, but I wanted to include a chapter on being a podcast guest. Not only are indy authors who are interested in having their own podcast usually interested in appearing on others' podcasts as well, but a consideration of the guest experience can be a useful exercise for a host. Perhaps every cruise ship captain should have the experience of being an anonymous guest on their own ship so that they can accurately gauge the experience their passengers are having.

Determining Your Destination

As with the decision whether to start your own podcast, you need to consider what your desired destination is, and whether being a guest on a certain podcast will help you reach it. Will a guest appearance help you along your desired course? In Part 2 - Determining Your Destination, I shared the three goals I have for *The Indy Author Podcast*: establishing connections with guests, building community with listeners and viewers, and creating income. I use these same criteria for assessing the benefits of being a podcast guest.

The opportunity to establish a connection with the host of the podcast is clear, and that podcast will reach a different audience, thereby continuing to build my own community. The potential of a podcast guest appearance to support income creation goals is a bit trickier but adding podcast appearances to your résumé will mark you as a professional and could pave the way to income creation opportunities.

Preparing for Your Voyage

In Part 3 - Preparing for Your Voyage, we discussed some factors you need to consider when preparing to launch your own podcast. Every podcaster has made these decisions—some more intentionally than others—and you need to consider if the host's choices make that podcast a good fit for you as a guest. Whether you are pitching yourself as a guest or are considering whether to accept an invitation from another podcaster, make sure you and the podcast and host are a good match for each other. (And, if you're pitching, make it easy for them to learn about you by providing appropriate information, including a link to an online press kit.)

Is the **topic area** of the podcast a good fit for your area of expertise? Is the host proposing a specific topic for the episode that interests you, and that you believe will fill, but not overfill, the time available? In case a host doesn't have a topic in mind, or is flexible on the topic, have a list of a few topics you are well-equipped to discuss so you can offer options. If you have a website, post these on an online press kit page. (You can link to my online press kit for The Indy Author in the More Resources section below.)

Is the **format** one that you will be comfortable with? I

would be less likely to accept an invitation to a roundtable podcast than an interview podcast because I like a more structured format and the one-on-one connection with the interviewer. (If you are pitching to a podcast, make sure that the pitch makes sense with their format—don't waste time pitching yourself as a guest to a podcast with a solo format.)

What's the podcast's **mode, medium, and venue**? Will the interview be live or recorded, available in video or audio-only, and are you sufficiently comfortable with those options? Is the venue in person or virtual and, if in person, is it logistically reasonable for you to participate?

What are the podcast's **deliverables, schedule, and structure**? Is the podcaster publishing episodes regularly (and so may have a larger and more loyal audience), and are they presenting those episodes in an attractive way (for example, with transcripts)? Do they have a regular structure to their episodes that you should be aware of so that you can feel comfortable with the content that will surround your portion?

What **persona** is the podcast host cultivating? Is the podcast clean or explicit? If clean, will you be willing to comply with that? If explicit, will you be comfortable with that? Consider if the tone of the podcast and host is a good fit. If you are a formal, reserved person, consider how comfortable you will be appearing on a podcast that has a very informal tone or that tends to discuss highly personal topics.

Does the podcast have a **brand livery** you should be aware of? If a host loves to use nautical metaphors, it would be fun to go into the interaction armed with a few you can use.

Is the **technology** of the podcast something you're willing to accommodate? Perhaps the set-up seems too complicated, or so basic that it suggests that the host isn't sufficiently focused on audio quality.

Finally, is the host bringing a spirit of **professionalism** to the podcast? If the podcast audio is bad, if the co-hosts talk over each other, if the accompanying website is out of date or contains typos, think twice about associating yourself with that podcast. This is especially important if the interview will be live. It's not likely that the interview they conduct with you will be coincidentally well run, or that their promotion of your episode will be coincidentally effectively performed.

Pitching Yourself as a Guest

Once you've decided that a podcast is a good match for you and your goals, you're ready to compose your pitch letter. Below are two pitch letters I received for The Indy Author Podcast.

This one (which I've reproduced in its entirety) resulted in an instant "thank you anyway."

Hi, I would like to be a guest and talk about <u>*topic*</u>*. I would also like to have you as a guest on my podcast to talk about your podcast.*

Even I don't think that talking about my podcast would make an interesting podcast topic.

The following pitch from Nat Connors of Kindletrends resulted in an immediate acceptance.

Hi, Matty, my name's Nat, and I run an author data newsletter called Kindletrends. I've just been listening to your podcast series with Orna Ross from ALLi, in particular the marketing and promotion episodes, and I thought you might be interested to hear about what I'm doing.

Briefly, I give authors and publishers on the Kindle Store weekly and monthly data to speed up their research: cover montages, summaries of what content is popular in particular genres, and downloadable data for optimizing their own ads, covers, and blurbs.

Technically it's a mixture of data visualization and natural language processing (for instance, figuring out first- vs third-person in blurbs), but I am very strong on cutting out technical jargon and keeping everything accessible. Kindletrends is designed to be timely, focused, and actionable. Everything in the newsletter is there because it makes a difference to real publishing decisions.

If you'd like to see an example, here's last week in the Teen & Young Adult Top 100, and this is the monthly summary for Mystery, Thriller & Suspense.

Weekly summaries are a summary of what's happened in the Top 100 charts this week—a little like the *Wall Street Journal* for working fiction authors—while monthly summaries support more in-depth analysis of the market, and identifying what themes are really resonating with readers. My goal is to produce a resource that's valuable no matter how much time someone has. If you have 30 seconds, then you can skim the Week in Summary section and get key facts. If you have more time, then the newsletter is your jumping-off point for the rest of your research for the week: down-loadable resources, web tools, and links to the store.

I've been on a few podcasts and given a few talks recently about genre research: Sacha Black's Rebel

Author Podcast as well as the Romance Writers of New Zealand's conference and ALLi's SelfPubCon.

If you'd like to learn more about Kindletrends, I'd be more than happy to give you a freebie coupon so you can see it for yourself. This is never going to be a huge business for me, but feedback from my author colleagues has been really lovely and positive; I do believe it's making a difference for working writers.

Thanks for your time,

Nat

Why did this merit an instant acceptance?

Nat demonstrated familiarity with my podcast by referencing specific guests and episodes. (In fact, if I receive a pitch that sounds interesting but feels like a form letter, sometimes I ask them which episode of The Indy Author Podcast is their favorite and why.)

He suggested a specific topic that would clearly appeal to my audience. (Something general like "sharing some tips and tricks I've learned as an indy author" wouldn't have worked as well because that would have meant I had to narrow the topic myself—the more work you can do for the podcaster, the better.)

He gave a concise description of the proposed topic, including samples and even free access to his paid service (not requiring me to pay to find out more about it).

He provided social proof by linking to his appearances on other podcasts that would appeal to the same audience as my podcast.

He made it easy for me to access appropriate materials by providing links. (Remember, don't make the podcaster have to work to find out about you!)

He closed with a focus on the benefit his topic can bring to my audience (rather than on himself).

Change of Plans?

Be thoughtful of the fact that the podcaster has set this time aside for you. If you can't meet at your scheduled time, give the podcaster plenty of warning—you don't want them to go through what might be a complicated set-up for the interview and then have to dismantle it if you notify them at the last minute. This holds true if you're sick—I'm only speaking for myself (and as a podcaster than records interviews weeks before their planned air dates), but I would rather hear from a guest the day before the scheduled interview that they aren't up for what I hope to be an energized discussion than to hear a few hours (or minutes) before our scheduled slot.

Setting Sail

Once you've accepted or landed a podcast guest appearance, many of the best practices described in Part 4 - Setting Sail— treating the space in which the conversation will take place to achieve optimal audio quality, honing your audio and video presence, making sure you've turned off computer and phone notifications during the event—will apply. In addition, you can do the host a favor by applying the same strategy of content reuse as you would for your own podcast: share the content widely within the parameters allowed by the host.

Below are a couple of final thoughts about having a successful guest appearance:

One way in which your preparation for a guest appearance might differ from your preparation for a host appearance is the "livery" or branding you reflect. For example, when I am hosting an episode of *The Indy Author Podcast*, I wear understated clothes and minimal jewelry because I want the focus to be on my guest. Similarly, my background is quite plain (nautical maps or a picture with a nautical theme, which are understated enough not to be visually distracting). However, if I'm appearing as a guest on a podcast that includes video, I wear brighter colors and am more likely to add accessories like jewelry or scarves. I also switch to the other side of my desk so that the background is the room rather than a wall, giving the viewers a little more of a sense of me personally.

Don't respond to questions with "That's a good question." I suspect most interviewees say this not because they think a question was particularly good, but because they are buying a few seconds to think of a response. The problem is that if you respond to every question with "that's a good question," it's meaningless. If you respond to only some of the questions with "that's a good question," then the interviewer may start to wonder what's wrong with the questions that don't get that response. If a question is truly noteworthy and you want to acknowledge it as such, reply with a more specific, and therefore meaningful, description—for example, "That's one I haven't heard before!" or "That really gets to the heart of the matter." If you're using "that's a good question" to buy some time, feel free to take that time in silence—no one is going to begrudge you a few seconds to formulate a thoughtful response to a question.

Captain's Log

You can capture your answers to these questions in the down-loadable worksheet available at TheIndyAuthor.com Podcasting for Authors.

What are five podcasts to which you'd like to pitch yourself as a guest, and what topic would you propose for the discussion?

What topics do you want to present as ones you'd like to address as a podcast guest? Do you have a public-facing platform, such as a website, where you can post these?

How might your brand livery differ when you are a guest versus when you are the host?

More Resources

To see The Indy Author online press kit, go to TheIndyAuthor.com Press Kit.

Links to the following resources are available at TheIndyAuthor.com Podcasting for Authors:

Audio for Authors by Joanna Penn, The Creative Penn

PART 5
EMBARKING ON THE VOYAGE

"Now bring me that horizon."

CAPTAIN JACK SPARROW

EMBARKING OF THE VOYAGE - LAST THOUGHTS

"The wind and the waves are always on the side of the ablest navigator."

EDMUND GIBBON

You have now determined your destination, prepared for your voyage, and are ready to set sail. The final chapter in this book, "Resources," summarizes those resources referenced at the ends of the chapters.

However, I'd like to return once more to those questions I posed at the end of each chapter, the answers to which serve as the Captain's Log for your podcasting voyage. Before we bring this leg of our journey to a close, I thought it might be helpful for you to see **my own Captain's Log for *The Indy Author Podcast***.

Why Podcasting ... and Why for Authors?

What about podcasting as an author appeals to you?

Listening to podcasts has become one of the primary ways that I keep up with developments in the writing and publishing worlds, and I'd like to provide that value to the followers of The Indy Author. I also agree with J. Thorn that "there's an intimacy to podcasting that doesn't exist in any other medium, including the written word," and I believe that intimacy will support the goals I have for *The Indy Author Podcast* (more on that below).

Determining Your Destination – Introduction

What are your goals for your podcast?

I want to use *The Indy Author Podcast* to establish connections with guests (so that my listeners and I can benefit from their expertise), to build a community with listeners (both to have a like-minded audience to whom to pay it forward and to support my financial goals), and to open opportunities for direct and indirect income creation.

How do you foresee those goals might change over time?

I foresee using the podcast as a "business card" for other income creation activities: offering consulting to authors considering launching a podcast, writing articles for traditional market publications, and garnering speaking engagements.

Establishing Connections with Guests

Who are your "most desired" guests for your podcast?

I have been fortunate to have hosted many of my most desired guests, many of whom are the podcasters to whom I have dedicated this book: Mark Leslie Lefebvre, Joanna Penn, J. Thorn, Zach Bohannon, Dale L. Roberts, and Jerri Williams.

They have already provided me with introductions to many other fantastic guests, and I feel certain that the network that *The Indy Author Podcast* has enabled me to develop will continue to open paths to many more.

Building Community with Listeners

What are your favorite podcasts, and what about them makes them so? How can you act on that knowledge for your own podcast?

The podcasts I listen to regularly are Mark Lefebvre's *Stark Reflections on Writing and Publishing*, Joanna Penn's *The Creative Penn* Podcast, and J. Thorn and Zach Bohannon's various offerings. I am also a regular beneficiary of Dale L. Robert's *Self-Publishing with Dale* YouTube channel. I appreciate the professionalism that they bring to their work and the personal experience and insights they share in order to smooth the writing and publishing voyages for their listeners. I appreciate the care they take in selecting expert guests whose knowledge will be helpful to their audience. Finally, I appreciate their commitment to interacting with their followers—all of them have gone beyond the call of duty in the support they have provided to me on my own creative and professional journeys.

What are podcasts you've tried and abandoned, and what prompted you to do so? How can you act on that knowledge for your own podcast?

Although I won't name names, the podcasts I have abandoned are ones where the host seems unprepared or where the information provided seems inaccurate or even unethical. I'm also not a fan of podcasts with more than two people (two co-hosts or one host and a guest) because "too many captains on the bridge" can sometimes cause the conversation to be disjointed or even to take on a somewhat competitive tone as the multiple hosts vie for airtime.

Creating Direct Income with Your Podcast

Is direct income creation a goal for your podcast?
Yes.

If yes, which of the direct income creation strategies we've discussed—patronage, affiliate income, and sponsorships—will you pursue?

I pursue patronage through Patreon and Buy Me a Coffee. I pursue affiliate and sponsorship income by recommending products and services that I use and that I believe offer value to my fellow authors.

If you're interested in affiliate income or sponsorships, what relationships will you pursue?

My current affiliate relationships include the Alliance of Independent Authors, Amazon, Aweber, Canva, Descript, Draft2Digital, Jane Friedman's *The Hot Sheet*, ProWritingAid, QuickBooks, ScribeCount, Scrivener, and Vellum. (You can access my affiliate links at TheIndyAuthor.com/Affiliates.) These are also the companies with whom I'd pursue sponsorships.

Creating Indirect Income with Your Podcast

Is indirect income creation a goal for your podcast?
Yes.

If you're interested in indirect income creation by using your podcast to introduce your listeners to your other offerings, what are those offerings, and do they tie logically to the proposed topic of your podcast?

I use *The Indy Author Podcast* to promote my books

(including *The Indy Author's Guide to Podcasting for Authors*) and my consulting service for authors considering launching a podcast. I also use it to pave the way for articles in traditional market publications and speaking engagements.

Preparing for the Voyage - Introduction

In addition to this book, what are some other podcasting resources you might tap into as you prepare for your voyage?

I have listed them at TheIndyAuthor.com Podcasting for Authors!

Choosing Your Topic

What is the topic upon which you want to base your podcast?

The Writing Craft and the Publishing Voyage

What are two dozen topics which might form the basis of individual episodes?

Check out my episode list at TheIndyAuthor.com Podcast.

Choosing Your Format

Which podcast format most appeals to you, and why?

Since I want to have complete control over the strategic and tactical aspects of my podcast, I knew I wanted to be a solo host. Since one of my goals was to tap into the knowledge of subject matter experts in the writing and publishing worlds, I chose an interview format.

Choosing Your Mode, Medium, and Venue

Will your episodes be live or recorded? What's the most important consideration for your choice?

The Indy Author Podcast is recorded because I value the additional control it gives me over the episodes and their content. The knowledge that I can address any snafus during the edit makes the experience of recording an interview more comfortable for me and my guests.

Will your episodes be audio-only or video? What's the most important consideration for your choice?

I always conduct interviews with my guests using video in order to benefit from the non-verbal cues one loses in an audio-only mode. *The Indy Author Podcast* episodes are available in video as well as audio (unless a guest requests that I not publish video). Video provides attention-getting fodder for promotional material.

Will your episodes be in-person or virtual? What's the most important consideration for your choice?

Although I conducted the early interviews for *The Indy Author Podcast* in person, I now conduct all my interviews using Zoom. A virtual interview greatly eases the logistics for me and my guests, enables more control over the recording environment, and means that I can draw my guests from anywhere in the world.

Choosing Your Deliverables

What steps will you take to ensure that you can provide high-quality audio to your listeners?

I have followed expert podcaster advice regarding equipment and room treatment to achieve optimal audio quality.

What other deliverables will you provide when you launch your podcast?

I provide audio and video of the episodes, as well as a complete transcript of the interview. I include applicable links in the show notes. I excerpt video clips from the interview to use as promotional material on Facebook, Twitter, and YouTube.

What materials will you produce as a normal part of your podcast that will interest your audience, and that you could produce with little to no additional time and effort?

At this time, there are no materials that I am producing as a normal part of the podcast that I am not already providing to listeners.

What additional deliverables might you consider adding over time?

At this time, there are no additional deliverables I am considering adding. If I were starting a podcast now, I would launch without the transcript and add that later if it seemed desirable.

Choosing Your Schedule

List the top podcasts in your niche and on what day of the week new episodes air. Based on this information, on what day will you post new episodes of your podcast?

Of the writing and publishing-related podcasts I listen to (noted above), none regularly publishes on Tuesdays, so I chose that day as the publish day for *The Indy Author Podcast*.

Choosing Your Episode Structure

What will the structure of your episodes be when you start out?

The structure of *The Indy Author Podcast* is:

- Standard podcast intro
- Episode-specific intro (including Patreon call to action and personal thanks to new Patreon and Buy Me a Coffee patrons)

- Personal update, including upcoming events and appearances
- Recommended resource (a sponsor, an affiliate, or one of my own offerings)
- Guest interview
- Interview wrap-up (including a question to spur interaction with listeners)
- Buy Me a Coffee call to action
- Standard podcast outro

What components might you consider adding over time?

I may expand my personal update and may add a segment commenting on news in the writing and publishing worlds.

Choosing Your Persona

Will you provide personal updates on your podcast? If yes, what type of information will you share? What will be off-limits?

The personal updates I provide on *The Indy Author Podcast* relate to my own writing and publishing work. Events in my personal life outside those areas are off-limits as topics, as is discussion of anyone else's personal life.

Will your podcast be clean or explicit?

Clean

If explicit, what are the language and topics you will incorporate that will give it this rating, and what might that mean in terms of the audiences to which you promote your podcast?

Not applicable for *The Indy Author Podcast*

Choosing Your Livery (a.k.a. Branding)

Do you have a brand you want to project, or one you would like to develop?

I interject nautical metaphors for the writing craft and the publishing voyage into the podcast, and The Indy Author nautically themed logo serves as the cover art for the podcast.

What livery will you use to do that?

I use nautical maps or nautically-themed pictures, which are understated enough not to be visually distracting, as my background for the podcast video. I also work to keep the focus on my guest by wearing understated clothing and accessories.

Choosing the Tech

What technology will you use for the following components of your podcast, or what additional research do you need to do before making a selection?

Computer - MacBook Air

Microphone and Earbuds - Blue Yeti USB microphone and non-mic-equipped earbuds

Online Meeting Platform - Zoom

Audio and Video Editing and Transcription - Descript

Podcast Hosting Platform - Libsyn

Setting Sail - Introduction

What does professionalism mean to you, and how will you act on that in your podcast?

Professionalism means creating a plan for my podcast, working diligently on executing that plan, and leaving nothing to chance. It means being respectful of my guests' and my audience's time and attention, and making sure they get as much value from the experience as I do.

Lining up Guests

Who are five guests you will invite to the early episodes of your podcast?

The next five guests I have scheduled for *The Indy Author Podcast* are experts in how to build a resilient indy business, futurist trends we can prepare for now, how analysis of movies and TV can improve our writing, how much it costs to self-publish a book, and the pros and cons of pre-orders.

To what additional guests might they be able to provide introductions?

One upcoming guest is affiliated with the Alliance of Independent Authors, and I will ask him if he has any recommendations for other guests from ALLi who would be a good match for *The Indy Author Podcast.*

Preparing for the Episode

Having one of your target guests in mind, what research will you do before you approach them about being on your podcast?

Before approaching the potential guest about an episode devoted to the pros and cons of pre-orders, I re-listened to an episode of another podcast where he discussed that topic. That enabled me to include references to that information in my invitation email.

If they accept, what additional research will you do before the interview?

In advance of the interview about the pros and cons of pre-orders, I will do some additional online research about what other industry experts have to say about pre-orders.

Creating the Environment

What steps can you take to make the environment where you will record your podcasts as conducive to high-quality audio as possible?

In addition to treating the room (surrounding my desk with room dividers, putting blankets over nearby hard surfaces), I also put my dogs in a room where they can't look outside and see a squirrel or deer that needs to be chased away by vigorous barking.

What sounds exist in the environment that might need remediation?

Since my neighbor is a lawn care fiend, I make sure all the windows are closed to reduce any noise from mowers or blowers.

If you will record video, what do you want in your background to support the persona you want to project?

I record in front of a wall decorated with nautical maps or other nautically-themed pictures.

What do you want to make sure does not appear in the background?

Because of the set-up I use for recording interviews for *The Indy Author Podcast,* I don't need to worry about what will appear in the background. However, since I use a different set-up for podcasts where I am the guest, I check to make sure that the curtain that separates the recording space from the neighboring room is closed, and that room dividers block the view of a dresser.

Refining Your Audio and Video Presence

Do you have experience listening to yourself in audio recordings or watching yourself on video? (If no, create some recordings in the medium you plan to use for your podcast and review them.)

After having listened to myself through dozens of episode edits, as well as other audio and video events in which I've participated, I've grown used to the sound of my voice and my appearance in video.

Are there any actions you want to take to address any self-consciousness about your audio or video presence that will remove it as a barrier to starting your own podcast?

I need to remember to sit up straight in order to avoid what may appear as a combative posture.

Creating the Episode

What might you want to change or add in your own flight checklist?

If I think of items to add, I'll update the checklist that I have shared with you!

What is one thing you want to be sure to keep in mind during your interactions with your guests (for example, Keep the focus on the guest)? (You can jot this on a sticky note and attach it to your monitor as a reminder during the live event or recording.)

Sit up straight!

Making the Most of Your Content

Based on how evergreen or time-bound your podcast content will be, over how long a time will you be able to continue to share that content so that you, your guests, and your audience get full value from it?

Most of the content of *The Indy Author Podcast* is evergreen, and I periodically review my backlist for information that I can re-share with listeners and viewers.

Making It Interactive

On what platforms (for example, social media, your website, YouTube) will you interact with your listeners?

I interact with listeners and viewers of *The Indy Author Podcast* on Facebook and Twitter, and direct them to YouTube to post comments on specific episodes.

Can you commit to replying to every comment your listeners post?

Yes.

Reducing Friction (Improving Your Production Process)

What mechanisms (for example, checklists, templates, etc.) will you use to help reduce the effort to create the podcast while still keeping the quality of the product high?

I will continue to refine my Excel-based task list, as well as the document I use to coordinate my work with my podcast assistant, to ensure the process is as streamlined as possible.

How long do you think it will take for the benefits you are enjoying from your podcast to begin to outweigh the cost of the time, money, effort, and stress of its production?

From a personal point of view, the benefits I am accruing from the podcast already outweigh the effort I put into it! The financial benefits from patronage are increasing gradually, and the podcast has paved the way for several paid speaking engagements and article placements.

Being a Podcast Guest

What are five podcasts to which you'd like to pitch yourself as a guest, and what topic would you propose for the discussion?

To promote *The Indy Author's Guide to Podcasting for*

Authors, I plan to pitch myself as a guest to podcasts targeting indy authors. I don't want to jinx myself by naming them here.

What topics do you want to present as ones you'd like to address as a podcast guest? Do you have a public-facing platform, such as a website, where you can post these?

Podcasting for Authors ... Creating Income and Connecting with Readers Using Short Fiction ... Indy Publishing in a Nutshell ... The Seven Processes of Publishing. I have captured these in my online press kit at TheIndyAuthor.com Press Kit.

How might your brand livery differ when you are a guest versus when you are the host?

I wear brighter clothes and more accessories such as jewelry when I appear as a guest. In addition, unlike my approach as a podcast host, where my focus is on drawing information out of my guest, I accept that the content I have to share will be the key factor in whether that audio or video experience has value for the listeners and viewers. Keeping that in mind, I also try to draw the host or interviewer into the discussion as appropriate.

AND NOW YOU'RE ready to get underway! Please drop me a note at matty@mattydalrymple.com and let me know how your voyage is progressing. You can also sign up for my email newsletter at TheIndyAuthor.com About & Contact.

I also hope to have a chance to interact with you via the episode comments for *The Indy Author Podcast*.

Good luck ... and may your podcasting voyage be a satisfying one!

LOOKING FOR A PILOT FOR YOUR PODCASTING VOYAGE?

I love helping fellow authors embark on and succeed in their podcasting voyage, and if you go to TheIndyAuthor.com Podcasting for Authors you can find lots of information on this topic, including my book *The Indy Author's Guide to Podcasting for Authors* and a number of free, downloadable resources. You can also find out more about my consulting services.

Using your answers to the questions included in the downloadable "Captain's Log" document available at that page, I work with you to **determine your desired podcasting destination, prepare for your podcast launch, and navigate your podcasting voyage**.

Client Dr. John Dentico says:

Matty helped me understand the ins and outs of starting and sustaining a straightforward quality podcast even when my original ideas and format were not the right mix. Her advice was invaluable, helping me simplify my approach and enabling me to produce a quality podcast.

Go to TheIndyAuthor.com Podcasting for Authors for more information, and for other resources that can support your podcasting voyage.

If podcasting is a creative dream you want to pursue, I hope you'll allow me to join you on that voyage!

RESOURCES

"It's not the towering sail, but the unseen wind that moves the ship."

PROVERB

I have consolidated the resources referenced at the end of each chapter here.

From The Indy Author

TheIndyAuthor.com Podcasting for Authors (including information on my podcasting for authors consulting services)

TheIndyAuthor.com Podcast For Guests of The Indy Author Podcast

TheIndyAuthor.com Press Kit

From The Indy Author Podcast

The Indy Author Podcast Episode 34 "Connecting through Video with Dale L. Roberts"

The Indy Author Podcast Episode 45 "Nine Things Career Authors Don't Do" with J. Thorn"

The Indy Author Podcast Episode 51 "Podcasting as Content Marketing with Jerri Williams"

Other Podcasts

The Creative Penn Podcast with Joanna Penn, including "Audiobook Narration, Production And Marketing Tips" with Derek Doepker

Stark Reflections on Writing and Publishing with Mark Leslie Lefebvre

Self-Publishing with Dale with Dale L. Roberts, including this discussion I had with Dale on his YouTube channel on "Podcast For Writers: How to Start a Podcast for Beginners"

Podcasting for Authors mini-series podcast with Joshua Rivers

Patronage Platforms

Patreon patron membership platform

Buy Me a Coffee patron membership platform

Other Podcasting Resources

Links to the following resources are available at TheIndyAuthor.com Podcasting for Authors:

9 Things Career Authors Don't Do: Podcasting by J. Thorn

Audio for Authors by Joanna Penn

Other Author Resources

You can find information on author resources and tools not specific to podcasting at:

TheIndyAuthor.com Resources
TheIndyAuthor.com Tools

ALSO BY MATTY DALRYMPLE

The Indy Author's Guide to Podcasting for Authors: Creating Connections, Community, and Income

ABOUT THE AUTHOR

Matty Dalrymple podcasts, writes, speaks, and consults on the writing craft and the publishing voyage as The Indy Author. She is the host of *The Indy Author Podcast* and the author of *The Indy Author's Guide to Podcasting for Authors*. She is also the co-author, along with Mark Leslie Lefebvre, of *Taking the Short Tack: Creating Income and Connecting with Readers Using Short Fiction*. Matty is a member of the Alliance of Independent Authors. Learn more at TheIndyAuthor.com.

Matty is also the author of the Ann Kinnear Suspense Novels *The Sense of Death*, *The Sense of Reckoning*, *The Falcon and the Owl*, *A Furnace for Your Foe*, and *A Serpent's Tooth*; the Ann Kinnear Suspense Shorts, including *Close These Eyes* and *Sea of Troubles*; and the Lizzy Ballard Thrillers *Rock Paper Scissors*, *Snakes and Ladders*, and *The Iron Ring*. Matty and her husband, Wade Walton, live in Chester County, Pennsylvania, and enjoy vacationing on Mt. Desert Island, Maine, and in Sedona, Arizona, locations that serve as settings for Matty's stories.

Matty is a member of International Thriller Writers and Sisters in Crime.

Go to www.mattydalrymple.com About & Contact for more information and to sign up for Matty's occasional email newsletter.

www.ingramcontent.com/pod-product-compliance
Lightning Source LLC
Chambersburg PA
CBHW071234210326
41597CB00016B/2043